SDB

My Testimony

Shella D. Bridgeman

Copyright © 2013 By Shella D. Bridgeman

All Rights Reserved

Published By: Shella D. Bridgeman

ISBN-13:978-0692309810

ISBN-10:0692309810

Please forward comments and requests to:

WWW.SHELLADBRIDGEMAN.COM

SHELLA@SHELLADBRIDGEMAN.COM

To the man who helped me to reach my level.

And you know who you are.

*Truly,
Your Queen*

~ In the spirit of the movie Love Jones ~

July 1, 2012—Sunday—1:04am

In my editing I had to figure out or truly consider my purpose for this book. This is what I used to guide me through deciding what to tell and not to tell. It is my story, but in telling it I had to share information about others. I tried to keep the truth in it and leave out parts that were really not relevant or essential to my point or message. I touched it up as best I could without changing the actual story. This is one of the hardest and most important things I've ever done in my life. I hope it will inspire others.

I feel like this is the child I never gave birth to. You do the best you can with good intentions and all that you know—along with giving it a part of yourself. This is my child. It has my DNA and it's a culmination of all of my experiences in my life. This is a product of me.

I'm doing the best I can with her. I just hope she will go out into the world and serve a purpose of good. She is what I've lived for, sacrificed for, loved for and I hope she makes it all worth it. She is my love child. I won't say she was an early baby or a late one. I'll just say she came when it was her time to come—when she was ready.

Hopefully a child comes when it is developed enough that it can live on its own outside of its mother's body. I believe she is ready and strong enough to stand on her own. She will not need my help to do her work. I have given her life. Now she will go out into the world and create her own place.

This is my child, my hope, my dream come true. I could not have asked for anything better or anything more. She is mine and she came from me so I accept her fully. She is mine. But she is also my gift that I give to the world as thanks for letting me hang out here with you. Thanks for putting up with me and giving me the time, space and patience to let me grow into who I was meant to be—just Shella.

Truth Is Freeing

February 2, 2003

This journal is a gift to me from my beloved aunt. She is a legacy of my father who also loved me very much.

I am so happy that for all I have experienced in my life - the one thing, has not been feeling that either of my parents did not love me. I believe anything else I can overcome. I have been crying today, as I have had the time to stop and think about a few things. The tears have really helped me. I feel a bit more relieved. After being pregnant and losing my baby and being married and being beaten and showing up for class in a room full of White people and them not understanding I was sick—all I could think to myself was—why does this have to be so hard?

I am in a lot of pain that I have not had the time to deal with because I have had to keep it moving. I miss my friend Christine as she is a gem. I have been alienated from her as a process of my husband's which fits right into his plans.

He could have been anything—a playwright, singer, comedian, surgeon and I'm sure there is more, but he chose the dark side.

I am my mother's daughter and I keep this new found picture of her close by to remind me of my strength. There is no one to talk to right now—as they would only make me put energy into an area where I don't want it. I am hurting right now and tears come to my eyes as I write these words and I think—will my face ever fully heal from that beating I received on Christmas Day? If my classmates only knew, but I realize we are so different that I must keep it all to myself. I have Buddy (my stuffed animal) and he will give me all of the comfort I can manage right now. He will even make it seem like I'm getting a hug.

February 3, 2003

I had a breakthrough today with Dr. Washington. She made me aware that I have functioned not as my real self for my entire adult life. She said I am intelligent, strong and moral. This is my soul and spirit and why have I lived outside of that?

Because I know of my true spirit I have struggled with myself as to how I make some of the decisions I make. She took this back as far as my childhood relationship with my older brother Bobby and discovered that is how I learned to be a victim. And because he lived in my house and was my brother, I learned to try and see the good in a person in order to help me to get through that situation.

This dichotomy has disturbed me greatly about myself. This even for me connects me to my trust issues. How could I live with my brother and not trust him? That past with him made me confused about who I should trust. This definitely ties into what allowed me to marry someone who had such a dark soul. She said it's not the acts a person commits that makes them good. It is the soul that is good or bad. Distorted actions make the soul bad. Would a person with a good soul intentionally hurt another person?

February 6, 2003

Today I have really said goodbye to my husband. I had my first session with Dr. Washington and she enlightened me greatly. I walked out of her door and felt the cool evening breeze. I came home and saw the glow on my face. I realize my strength cancels out my husband and I have no fear, therefore, we are not connected anymore. He will never see me again and I feel sad for that. That means I fear for his fate because of choices he has made. Dr. Washington said something to me that made me feel she believes what I feel about his fate. He created a really bad karma for himself. And for what I believe his fate is to be— it makes me sad and love him.

I can allow myself to love him because I know it is over. She also told me he is not a bad person, but he is being controlled by another spirit that has entered his body. He has admitted as much to me and that he fights it daily. As she stated, it would be a miracle if he could overcome this, which makes me think of his demise. He taught me a really great lesson. From here I will do the work I need to do to strengthen my spirit to live as who I really am. I will also learn to protect myself and catch up to where I am supposed to be in life. This is why my favorite saying is, I don't have time. It is because I don't. Just as my self-defense training may be learned—so it comes naturally...

My spiritual self-defense must come naturally also.

He really did love me, but it was so convoluted with so much other stuff, like his demons. His torture is knowing his demons got the best of him.

This lesson of the day is, always protect myself.

February 10, 2003

It is true that anything you do good in the physical world is good in the spiritual world. Today I physically let go of some items I no longer needed—and in turn my husband was taken into custody. He denied the whole thing to his parole officer and even seemed shocked when he was caught. I hope he owns up to this so he can start to heal himself. Let go of the things you don't need anymore and you'll be surprised what will happen next.

I realized today I was sexually abused by my husband. After meeting this very nice guy at the mall and talking with my girlfriend is when it came to me as to why I need to wait a long time before I can be intimate with anyone.

February 11, 2003

My epiphany of the day is, I can not move forward until I take care of the past. I realized this as I was trying to sort through all of the school work I need to complete. I realized I can not focus properly on the future until I take care of my unresolved business.

I stayed connected with myself all day today and was very productive even though I have been up since early this morning until late at night. I am not exhausted. I guess it's because I did not work against myself today. And even though I ran really hard today, it was good energy I exerted. I also realize all of the energy I was wasting on my marriage. The same energy can be so beneficial to me. Do I have any for anyone else? I have very little or it has to be very much a give and take relationship. It has to have something positive to offer me. This morning I woke up to a gentle hug, but I don't know who it was from. It felt really good. I want to start on my feet again, but I want to be sure I am going to keep them up. I spent a lot of time with myself today and the bath was good and relaxing.

February 13, 2003

I regret I gave him my phone number yesterday. I regret it because I just flung my door open to something I know is drama.

Today I realized I am going to have to really do the work to be okay. I soaked my special socks in bleach overnight and it didn't get rid of the dirt. It only got rid of the surface, meaning on the top, but there was still lots of black dirt on the bottom. I had to scrub to get the dirt out. I had tried to do it the quick and easy way, but it didn't work. In order to use those socks on my feet—I had to clean them before I could feel good about using them. This is representative of my life also.

Yesterday I was connected enough with myself to ask the right question. What was his daughter's name? It saved me a lot of drama.

February 15, 2003

I have already neglected my writing by one day. Maybe I was distracted by Isaac? We went out last night and had a great time, but I think he likes me. That makes me concerned. Our relationship horoscope says this relationship can help to heal old wounds, but I don't know if this is using him. I need to talk to my aunt about this. I don't want him to distract me. He says he will be my friend if I only want to talk. In talking with him I had to ask myself if I want to be a public or private person. Is it okay for him to be with me and spend money on me? Will I feel guilty or is that normal?

I think he will be a good friend to help me heal old wounds. Did God send him to me? I believe my decision to go to the concert with him was ultimately based on the fact that I enjoy his company. He makes me feel good. I decided to go with him and have something to share with someone.

I decided tonight I am going to budget my money and not work for this year and work on healing myself and doing well in school. I was tempted today to be intimate with my friend Troy. I believe I have to be strong enough to save him from himself. I believe I am my brother's keeper. Of all men, he could really tempt me. He is another one I think that should not have gotten married. I believe he cares about me outside of everything.

I wonder if a baby will ever come from my body.

February 17, 2003

Why am I still so bothered about the decision to go to the concert with Isaac? Is it because I'm not supposed to go with him or I chose to go with him for the wrong reason, like protection? He does kind of annoy me because I can feel he likes me. I can see him inviting me to one of his barbeques and I wouldn't want to go.

I had a dream about things I think Troy has put on my mind. My moral self says to not even consider it, but my ego and human self says to have an affair with him. I am also reminded that I may get married again and I wouldn't want some woman to do that to me. As bad as I know he would feel, I think I know he would sleep with me. She should not have married him because he was not ready and she wanted children. She must not be too bright or she really loves him. She doesn't even fully satisfy him. Never marry a person like that. You must be able to give yourself freely to your man so he doesn't have an excuse to cheat.

I also had a dream about my husband that I was having a

conversation with him and then he brought up his youngest son. At that point I realized he was trying to get in good with me—and I had to remember the scenes of him beating me in my face.

February 19, 2003

God please give me the strength to do the work I need to do. And God please don't let me think about anyone more than I do myself. Is it when I have to continue to wonder if I have made the right decision—that I have made the wrong one? God please give me strength.

I have decided to not work for the rest of this year as I am going to make this for the first time in my life a time when I will attend college with no distractions. I shaved my feet today hopefully for the last time. Can I be committed to keeping them up? By the end of this year I should have developed a constitution and be stronger in who I am. I should then have learned to create a barrier between me and the world, always protecting myself. I also realize today, as three is my number, I shall be pregnant one more time and this time it will be right. The first time I was pregnant was 13 years ago.

Tonight after class I came home and watched Soul Food. Bird had to or chose to confront a teacher who had slept with her as well as other girls while they were in high school. She had been feeling guilty for all of these years about him losing his job and getting beaten up by her father. She finally realized he deserved whatever he got. She stood up to him and told him if he ever contacted her again—she would mess up his life the way he had tried to do to her all those years ago—because what he did was wrong. She released herself from the guilt of his punishment he had received. <u>Because he was wrong</u>. She also resolved it for herself by facing him and telling him to his face. I should not have fear if I have to do this. And not feel guilty about anything that may happen to my soon to be ex-husband as a result of his actions. He tried to destroy my life. God have mercy on his soul. Music sang that song. Was it manipulation?

Being <u>present</u> in school tonight really made me feel like a superstar, on top of the world.

February 20, 2003

Today I realized it might be true that I immediately jump to the negative when something goes wrong. Today I automatically assumed the man was being dishonest with me when he told me it would take until Tuesday to get the papers served. Does this mean I am a negative person?

Douglas is a really smart man. I used what he told me regarding listening to people when they are drifting off. They usually make true statements. Like looking off into nothing and making a statement.

February 21, 2003—4:30am

Why does it feel like God took His hand and shook my shoulder as to say, hey? I don't know why I'm supposed to get up. Maybe it's to do my homework. But is there something somewhere that is not okay? I even wept and thought of my aunt, if she's okay. But I dare not call her. I also thought of things I wanted from her in case I never saw her again. I also thought about the things I needed to write down and she gave me this book to write them in. Am I doing like I said, jumping to the negative? Maybe I'm just afraid to lose her as I do get so much from her. Yesterday evening we sat down and had a pork chop dinner with applesauce and I love it when she blesses my food. She gives me more than she will ever know. God please don't let me lose her anytime soon.

February 23, 2003—6:02am

I had to take a break from studying to write down my light bulb moment, a phrase coined by Oprah. I remembered a conversation I had with my school psychologist mentor and she mentioned a study or research she was conducting on students at one of her schools. I started to say to her it was a longitudinal study, but I was afraid I might be wrong. It was on my mind while studying and I had to get up and check one of my books. I

WAS RIGHT. I am sure I am smart. So what is my problem? Where does the doubt come in at? It also tells me there is a lot of information stored away that is waiting to have the opportunity to come out. Over the last two days I have met three amazing women over the phone. They have all three provided me with information I really needed. The message I get from those experiences is there are people out there waiting to help. Let go and let God means I will be proactive in whatever I need to accomplish and release myself of the burden and let God carry me through what I need to accomplish.

Today is 2/23/03 and I am going to church with my aunt. I was feeling kind of overwhelmed as I have so much school work to catch up on. I guess I could be doing worse things than going to church today. But I really don't have time. I also have to go to a baby shower today which also affects my time issues, not to mention my lack of sleep. I figure this is the least I can do for two people I care a great deal for. But I can not make these sacrifices again anytime soon. My main focus is to get my life back on track and that is going to take all of my time and energy for a while.

I am also realizing how badly I was treated in my marriage as I now have discomfort from an infection. I was experiencing this monthly in my marriage and he never was concerned enough to let me heal. He dogged me and I let him. I will never think so little of myself again.

Also that dog my mother used to date has called me this morning and I know his intentions are no good. What a reality check on how men can be. You'll notice it if you just pay attention.

I also noticed Isaac is nothing like what I thought he was. How could a person that is anywhere present not know who the mayor is of the city they live in? He is definitely not on my level.

February 25, 2003

I realize this morning after evaluating our conversation from last night, we can't be friends. It's amazing what you can learn about a person when you take the time. I realize he often makes the distinction between him and myself being that he is stable and I'm not. Last night he even mentioned I have issues. Of course I corrected him by informing him I am just a busy person. My next move with him is to cut him off and I'll just have to figure out how I'm going to do that. He thinks he is better than me. Correction, he is another oppressive, abusive Black male. He knows he is not better than me. He is actually insecure, so he says these things to feel better about himself and to make me feel less than who I am.

Yesterday God sent me a woman who gave me some information that would help me. She also validated that my instructor Dr. Baker is insecure and controlling and wants to keep me in my place.

I need to make sure I follow my instincts when something doesn't sit right with me—just like when I asked Dr. Baker the question regarding giving feedback to parents. She should have told me about the consent form I needed to use for that process.

I believe I was led to Berkeley. In the confusion of fleeing my marriage I ended up here. It did not seem to make sense as it was so close to the place I left. Currently, I have been faced with challenges in school which have directed me to Berkeley as a place that can help me. I have questioned this as I am unsure if I want to be a public or private person. I believe the feeling of richness I want to come from my work lies in Berkeley—my true home.

In times of confusion I look at my mother's picture and I can feel when she is in agreement. I believe she is proud of me.

March 5, 2003

We have not talked for a few days as I have been so very stressed. Maybe that's the best time to do this, but I just couldn't. I had a breakthrough. The reason why I am always so apprehensive about speaking up when I have experienced an injustice is because my earliest experience of oppression came from my brother Bobby. How do you tell on your brother and still live together and he not hate you and how will you then protect yourself in the future? I obviously have some issues that need to be worked through.

Tonight in class after arriving for only an hour, I realized the strength within myself to overcome the White people. I have appeared very sketchy as I really have been. I've been impacted by all of the things pulling at me in my life. I believe I have had time to regroup and become ready to go back out there and fight. By the end of this month I will have caught up on all of my school work at my own pace and in my own way and then I'll be ready for new challenges.

On 3/3/03 my restraining order was put in place and he was served. I think I realized I can't talk about it anymore if I want to focus on moving ahead. I think talking about it gives it power. I am going to overcome. I am going to be Dr. Bridgeman. I actually got something done this morning. I finally cleaned my mirrors, the bathroom and the walls in the kitchen. I'm now going to get some rest and get ready for tomorrow.

March 6, 2003

After two months of cable drama—I have fixed my cable. I have had a phenomenal day today. I went to the place to buy a used TV where I bought one when I was leaving Berkeley. Now I'm buying one upon my return. And the one I bought from the man 14 years ago is still working. I just want a TV with a remote control for it.

He talked with me about a business development plan for Berkeley. He saw in me a person who is going somewhere. That's why he told me—I'm going to tell you this and if any day you find a way to use it.... Just as I was writing this my TV is turned to channel 64 the city's station and Mariah Carey's song Hero came on the TV. The message was— the hero lies in you.

It seems today that my life has come full circle. I now have the understanding of my book. The significance of the book will be that I'm from here, left, came back after being educated and I will educate my community and uplift it.

March 16, 2003

I miss my husband. I miss his lips, his kisses and the way he would sway me in his arms. I miss everything that was beautiful about us. I miss how there was no shame in his love for me. He would love me in public in front of everyone. I miss his jokes and his (What is that? and—hello). That will always be with me. I miss Jamison and Andrew and as I am afraid to write this on paper, I think one day they will come to me. They both know I loved their father and if they ever need to find me as they are their father's children, they will. Andrew truly loved me and he knows he is my son. When I was at Joy's baby shower her mother-in-law asked me if I had any children and I said no and just smiled. I did not mention to her the child I had just carried in my body and lost and the others I had mothered and lost. Andrew truly received all of my love and stored it somewhere in his body so he can retrieve it one day when he needs to.

I made my husband stand up a lot straighter because I was his. He wore that cheap gold band like it was the world. He loved me that much. We were like the perfect taste of brown sugar, caramel and white chocolate. All things that are sweet but in a different kind of way. My heart longs for the love we had. The love people saw when they looked at us. The love that was there when we looked into each other's eyes. The love was in the kiss and the hug.

I carried our child in my womb for almost two months, but she could not stay. Her name was Sara and she was beautiful. She had her father's complexion and her mother's smile and hair. She grew up to be lean and curvy and had legs like Sasha (my mother). She was smart, very outgoing, creative and good in sports. She was a beautiful person. People were happy with just being in her presence. She had a beautiful spirit and she was a charmer. When she smiled the room lit up. Her hair was long and black and thick and she was everything we could have hoped for and more. She was the perfect child her father had always wanted and she changed his life. She was a dream come true. We loved her so much. Her father didn't care much for the name Sara, but he loved it because he knew that was truly her name. The name he gave her was Pretty-Two or Too. This was because her mother was pretty. He may have been right when he said no one will love me like him. He did truly love me, but the bad part of him would not let him. It made him obsessive and controlling. He made love to me in the way he did because he wanted to be connected to me in a way that was impossible. He was constantly trying to get a piece of my spirit. My spirit turned him on and fed him. This is how he managed to always be ready. He finally snapped on me on Christmas Day because he was not able to tap into my spirit. I was not available to feed him. It's almost like a mother nursing her baby. Her body has to produce enough milk to feed the baby. That was what my sex was like for him. His food came from my body.

Three months later I finally cried. I have finally cried for all of the pain I have experienced. The loss of my baby, my husband, my children and my freedom. After talking with Harriet I have relieved myself of the burden that his blood will not be on my hands. He will get out of jail, but it is after that his demise will occur. She explained to me how badly he felt about hurting me. I do know him. The good him. I know the good him has a conscience and that's what keeps him up at night. I helped him to sleep. He needed me. I realize if he leaves this life before I do, then he will be one of those angels watching out for me. Then he will take care of me the way he wanted to. I pray for his soul as I know he is truly a good man but is tormented by all of the things of his past. I pray to God to please have mercy on his soul. I do forgive my husband for his actions. But I am angry at him and hurt because he has taken so much from me. I had the potential to have it all with him and he messed it up.

March 17, 2003

Tonight, I meet with Dr. Holloway and Dr. Ashley. Wish me luck.

March 27, 2003

I am finally sitting down with myself to talk some things out with myself. Of course I overcame the meeting with the bigwigs and I walked away thinking they don't believe I will succeed. This is what I think I will use as my motivation. I have been chipping away at my school psychology testing with the assistance of Dottie. She truly has a good spirit. I have noticed the subtle hints of how people don't want to help me. Their lips say I want to help you, but the logistics of what they are offering makes what I need not possible. I stood up big time on 3/26 which was my husband's 41st birthday. My usual routine of connecting with myself didn't work and I couldn't understand why. So I took a step I felt it was time for. I finally ended my relationship with Tracy. It felt really good. I had immediately cleared up enough space for me to go shopping and buy some food. I felt really good about how I did it because I did not say anything bad about her as to why I was ending the friendship. I asked her for my wedding pictures she said she threw away, but as I drove away from her house I realized I didn't need them because I did have one of him and that was enough. I also realize I will give my grandmother my P.O. Box number as a way to stay in touch with her and it also gives the family a way of contacting me if they need to. I do not trust my family. That is my reason for not connecting with them, but I want to know if she is alive or not.

I have also decided if anyone sends anything to that P.O. Box then I will write to them my feelings about them. I also realize I do not want anyone in my house. I will communicate with people mainly by e-mail which will suffice for me. I am truly being delivered. I forgot to mention after I ended the friendship with Tracy I got into my car and the song was playing on the radio my husband used to sing to me. In my heart because this generally happens at a good moment for me I feel it is him wishing me well. The times like after I saw Dr. Washington, when I found his social security number for my taxes, when I found my two chairs for $26, when I finally filed my divorce papers and when I ended my friendship with Tracy.

May 8, 2003

Hopefully I have taken the time to write down things about the times that have been challenging for me. It has been a while since I've written—at least a few weeks. Today I'm at the end of this challenge with school. I had to get all of my incompletes resolved in order to continue my studies. I'm almost there. It seems as though I had to have a fire lit under me in order to produce. Today I drove in my car home from the school and I started to wiggle a bit in my car. I noticed how uncomfortable that was for me. Not because I am still hiding from anyone, but because it has been so long since I've been happy. For all of the time I was married to that man I realize how stressed out I was. My nervous tick has finally stopped. My eye doesn't twitch anymore. It's a wonder I'm in school and I was able to hold it together at all. I also came home and turned on my music, lit an incense and poured a glass of wine. I haven't done any of this since I have moved into my new place. I must really be getting better. Last night at a time of stress, I picked up the book Harriet gave me and read some of it. I believe it has also helped me to feel better today. I talked to myself today in the mirror and told myself it is important to stay focused and take care of myself. Putting myself first does not mean I am being selfish it just means I am taking care of myself. I haven't done this for so long. I also realize I have possibly not valued myself as much as I should have because my mother didn't do it. She did not protect me from my brother and she knew that he was physically abusing me. This has allowed me to not protect myself from things that have been bad and dangerous for me.

I also realize I was so concerned about Barry I was not focused on what I should have been—me. If I had gotten things going with him I would not be where I am with almost finishing my work. If it is meant for me and him or anybody, I need to continue healing myself and it will come. I know in my heart I am not going to be alone and my next husband will come from my school and he will be everything I want and need.

Today I feel much stronger than I have been recently. I feel strong enough to face people and challenges. I also plan on facing the men in my past to prove to myself I can. Also I will resolve whatever allowed me to marry a man who was a combination of them all. This will be my closure. The next man will be totally different. He will be good. All of those men of my past have in common the fact that they mistreated and used me, but more importantly—I let them. I want to prove to myself I am so over that type of person and I am no longer vulnerable to that type of man. My ex-husband so felt like my first boyfriend and if I resolve things with him in turn I will be resolving things with my ex-husband.

I feel like coming back to Berkeley has given me the opportunity to resolve my past, so I can move forward in a good way.

I think I have decided her name will be Hope. In her I see hope for everything. Life will be good. There is always the possibility for good.

May 9, 2003

In reference to my feet and stuff, when you try to take a short-cut to remedy the problem it only comes back faster and worse. If you take your time to work on the problem it eventually goes away. But to keep it away you have to work on it regularly and sometimes that means daily.

The satisfaction is greater also when you take your time to work on a problem because you can see the results as you go. This makes you believe if you can resolve this problem that has plagued you for so long than you can accomplish anything. This knowledge comes to me from working on my feet.

May 12, 2003

Just after I made that last entry I heard that song again. I haven't heard it much recently because I haven't had many breakthrough moments. I have noticed when I hear that song it kind of distracts me and I start thinking about him a lot. And maybe that is exactly his reason for doing this. This tells me he is still tapped into me and knows very much what I'm doing, but the part I'm working on is being strong enough to handle anything and not have fear.

Since the baby I notice a different smell. I think my body chemistry is changing.

On the eve of my new found success I attribute it to taking off the cape. I took off the cape and realized I am only human. This allowed me to recognize my limits. When my feet began to swell that meant it was time to go to bed. Acknowledging these limits allowed me to go to bed and wake up more prepared for my task at hand. As I moved through the process of my work I realized it was not as hard as I thought it was. It only seemed that way because I was trying to do something that was impossible. The amount of work I was trying to do could not have been done overnight. It took the amount of time it took. I think the biggest step for me was realizing my limits. It actually helped me. This experience has brought me more to what Dr. Washington said about working with myself. If I—Shella Bridgeman, want to be successful, I can't rush. This process of work could not be rushed and in the process I was actually learning not just doing.

I looked at my feet today and it is amazing what some consistent work can do. The outsides of my feet look almost perfect, but the insides need more work. I attribute this same philosophy to me personally. The outside can be almost perfect, but the inside takes more work to repair.

Doing my schoolwork helps me to connect with myself and helps me to be quiet and okay with it. These are actually all of the behaviors I need in order to be successful at my schoolwork.

I feel just like my horoscope said, cleaning my closet and making room for the new stuff to come in. It's funny how when you're doing the right thing so much good comes from it. As I have been working so hard on my feet, my arms are being built up.

May 16, 2003

I think I have finally found out the connection between my neighbor and myself. I have noticed it has been quiet up there recently. Someone has been home, but there has been no loud noise like usual. I have also noticed their car that is parked next to mine never has anything in it. I understand my reason, because I don't want anyone to know anything about me. I also realize one day when I was leaving she would not back in because we then would have been face to face. Also one time when they were coming out neither person looked at me. I know he's on parole and he doesn't have a key because he has been calling to her from downstairs when he needs to get in. Is that her car? Is he the one that was making all of that noise? Is it her apartment? And has he gone back to jail? Is she another sista trying to make it and she married the wrong guy?

I think I have found an advocate in Dr. Lake. I think everything is going to be fine with school.

May 20, 2003

It takes a winner to come from behind. I sit here right now after finally making a move. I lie here for days stinking, thinking and watching TV. I realize this may be an emotional time for me as I may be having P.M.S. and I am still trying to finish my work for school. There is a part of me that believes all will be well with school because I am doing the best I can. I have taken some breaks because I had to take the time to reconnect with myself. I am really feeling like this is a critical time in my life and people who are not here for me now don't deserve the front row seat in my life. I am starting to figure out the role of family. They are the people who will be there for you so you need to make time to make a contribution to the family. I cried this Sunday because I wanted my aunt and the love of my family. I also realize the man I married was so close to the make-up of my first boyfriend. I question the future relationship with me and my mentor. I think it's most important for someone to be there at the critical times in one's life, like now. I can't think of a more important time than now. What kind of relationship do we really have, maybe a distant one?

The one I married and my first. The relationships felt the same. The same type of dysfunction. I can remember when I was pregnant and I told him there might be reasons why he didn't want me to be pregnant. I can remember the fear I had because he was waiting for me to say he couldn't afford the ones he had so why would he be happy about another one. I felt he wanted me to say it so he would have an excuse to get mad and hit me. But at the same time he told me about when Maryann was pregnant with Andrew—how he didn't want him and how it went bad. Andrew and Jamison were nine months apart because he did the same thing to her he did to me. He made me have sex with him just after I had lost my baby and I think he even took the condom off so he could try to get me pregnant again.

I paid for the wedding, the room for the honeymoon and both rings and the boutonniere he refused to wear.

May 24, 2003

I feel really connected with myself. I realize I must make time for my family not for them but for me. It is food for my soul to spend time with people who love me. In these recent trying days, I have taken the time to connect with my family and I notice it has made me feel better about my circumstances. I haven't spoken with them specifically about things I am experiencing, but somehow just talking with them helps me to feel better. They want me to be present at events because they want me around. Why would you want someone around if you don't like them? They like me. It's really true what they say about being loved and it helping you to feel better about yourself and more comfortable in the world. In spite of everything this instructor is putting me through it is making me feel better to know I have someone who cares about me—my family.

Jewel is another person who has been there for me and she truly wants me to be happy. Harriet sent me an e-mail yesterday about some FCC stuff. How crude is that? She has not even taken the time to check on me regarding other things. I am going to spend tomorrow and next Saturday with my family because they love me.

I think I am going to see Barry again this summer and I'll be in a better place. When I think of all of the feelings that crept up inside of me just from meeting him I am so amazed to know such a thing is possible. He touched my spirit. Meeting him was a beautiful feeling. He made my body feel love. Something Harriet said I think was true, that he felt the same thing. When I see him I am going to have the biggest smile on my face and it is going to be like seeing a long lost friend.

I notice my body is healing inside and out. My facial scar under my eye is almost gone and based on my monthly bodily experiences I am healing inside. Every month my body cleanses itself and every month he is leaving my body. I even smell fresher. I also don't know why I continue to worry about things because if I think back over all of my life experiences I have always made it through. Maybe it's like the Indiana Jones move—to dive on the floor and make it under the gate just before it closes, but I always make it. I guess this is where the faith comes in at—knowing everything will be okay.

May 24, 2003

I may be depressed because I notice I don't have an appetite for food. I guess I might have a reason as I don't have any money. I'm still working on this darn homework and I'm trying to stay positive in spite of everything.

May 26, 2003

In order to respect a man he has to be strong and in order to love a man he has to be weak. You respect him for his strength and love him for his weakness. Is this why I have loved so many men—because they have been weak, but I can't think of one I have respected.

May 30, 2003

It's a few days after the anniversary of my wedding and I am going through it. I am writing this half way intoxicated after one wine cooler and one twelve ounce Budweiser beer. This was all I could afford as I only have to my name less than twenty dollars with no gas in my car. I bought a loaf of bread and a quart of milk, some Certs and it took two trips to the store to acquire the Budweiser. I had a dilemma about whether or not to buy the alcoholic beverages as I have very little food in my house. But I needed to do something to help me to get rid of my headache from all of the stress I am experiencing. I have to wait until Monday to find out the results of my status with school. I have messed up in a big way by letting personal decisions get in the way of my academic pursuits. I think at this time I have decided to enlist in a battered women's support group because there is now an overlay to the way I function in life relating to how the abuse has affected me. I believe it has affected how I interact with other people and has helped to make me feel a bit insecure and unworthy.

I just woke up after being passed out from my wine cooler and Budweiser. I lay on the couch still trying to come up with some solutions regarding my situation. I couldn't come up with anything only the counseling I need. So I finally decided to turn on the TV and the scene from Men of Honor was on. Cuba Gooding, Jr. was under water for so long trying to assemble a mechanical part they made so difficult for him to accomplish. He finally assembled the part and came up with his face blue because the water was so cold. He then gave the instructor a look as to say, I don't care how hard you make this for me I am not going to quit. I clearly relate this to my current situation. Prior to this part of the movie it was also shown he had problems with his academics and had to work extra hard at them. He made the reference that he recognized his academic challenges, but he was meant to do this job.

Although I would not claim I am receiving the best education possible, I should not feel so inadequate about my training performance because we don't actually receive very much assistance with the work. Therefore, extra help you may need can be a mark against you if you ask for it.

I also make the correlation between Cuba's character and me with wanting to be the best. He is trying to achieve the highest level in his career and so am I. A big part of this whole thing—

is in order to be the best in my field I have to become Dr. Bridgeman. That's a big part of the significance of this university is because it is the only one in this area that offers this program.

Also referring to the movie, in extreme times of difficulty, there has to be something that drives you to continue.

In the movie there was a significant moment when he would either make it or not and someone believed in him and helped him.

I don't think I was too far from a good thing in marrying him because we were friends first. He was always a good friend to me. If we could have maintained the content of that relationship things could have been better. The conflict came because we were coming from two different worlds and trying to merge the two was very complicated. It could have worked if he had been stronger—strong enough to do his part and be honest, not prideful. If he had been focused and committed to the relationship everything else could have been worked out because I loved his children. He had not worked out enough of his stuff in order to help him see clearly in the relationship. Or did he enter into the relationship not willing to work on his stuff? Therefore, he was making me the fall guy for what he was not willing to do. The night before we got married, he said he was not ready, but I told him it would be okay. He tried to spare me from what he knew I might go through. He knew his own potential and knew exactly what would happen. He could not sustain the pressures of his new life and he ended up costing himself everything. Just like he said about the movie Disappearing Acts, Wesley Snipes was making false promises about working the three jobs if he had to in order to take care of his family. The funny thing about it is that was the same thing he said he would do in the beginning. He later admitted he had no intention of working that hard.

The mistake that was made was I was ready for marriage, but I knew he wasn't and I did it anyway. The mistake he made was he knew he wasn't ready and he did it anyway. We both made a mistake and we are both paying the price for our careless actions.

June 3, 2003

There is some relevance to not being high. You are then forced to make your situation better so you can breathe. I think it might be okay to have a day or two in extreme situations to help to take the edge off, so you can begin to move forward. But I can see the connection between pot users and them not resolving their stuff. It keeps you numb so you are never present enough to feel things in order to be forced to deal with them.

This past weekend I attended a family gathering in honor of Darren's recent graduation from Ohio State. Most of the people there were nice and it turned out to be a pretty nice day in spite of my previous thoughts. I was surprised to find out later about everything that was going on surrounding a married man I was talking to. Apparently, my cousin and his buddy were mad at the guy for even talking to me. I found out about this yesterday when we talked. It did not make me feel good that I was the center of something bad, but it did make me feel good when my cousin told me he had my back. It felt good. During the whole time at the picnic he was watching out for me and I didn't even know it. But again it wasn't just him it was his buddies also. He made me feel something I wish I had gotten from my brothers.

June 3, 2003

I have to take the time to thank my aunt. She is a wonderful woman. She gave me this beautiful book I am writing in. I don't know what she puts in her food, but everything is always good. I am really not a junk food junkie, but every cake and cookie she has ever made has left an after taste in my mouth that only makes me want more. I guess she came just when I needed her the most. There just doesn't seem to be enough of her to go around. She is supportive and loyal to everyone. She gives so much of herself with every cake, cookie, pudding and recipe. She often reminds me of me. A little tough and to the point, but she has a heart of gold and worries about everybody. That's why she fusses at us all of the time. Just like a true Gemini, give her a day and things look different and you <u>always</u> have to check her temperature to find out where she is. She has helped me to understand how people feel about me. We are both hard to figure out. She looked so proud of me the day she saw me bless my food.

June 12, 2003

I actually feel okay right now. I was quite distressed earlier today because I had to leave out of the house and go to school, schedule an appointment for school work, buy something for my aunt's birthday and visit with her. I was also kind of ticked off at that woman for not giving me my eight dollars back for those two chairs I bought from her. I came home, ate and took a nap. My aunt called and woke me up then I went to visit her and gave her flowers I had bought for her. She gave me a really strong hug as if she really appreciated them. I sat and watched her make two caramel cakes and my presence even helped her to get through the process as she was really tired. It turned out to be really nice and it was a way for us to spend some quality time together. Somehow just being there with her made me feel better about everything I am going through. It also made me feel like things tend to work themselves out.

When I was at school today I overheard Barry had been out on a date with another young lady from the school. Somehow it didn't hurt my feelings. It just gave me more insight as to how he is making himself into some type of joke of the school because the date didn't seem positive. Apparently there was something the young lady didn't know about him until the date was over, which was the same thing that happened with me. After the date is when he let me know he didn't want a relationship.

I have had some very trying days lately with my financial issues. But as I should truly know by now things do work out.

June 21, 2003

Well it's the day after my birthday and of course it was bad. I had no money, no gas in my car and only one person called me to wish me a happy birthday. I am kind of angry, kind of sad and still kind of reflecting on my life and trying to figure out what the heck is going on. What went wrong? What was it that happened and what might be coming next? Today, the day after, I felt a little better. I think a part of it is because I didn't have all of the pressure on me of being happy. I think I have committed to quitting smoking. I have come to this thought because I have no money and if I do need to ask someone for some, I don't want it to be for cigarettes. I also thought I might need to learn to exercise some self-control. That might be helpful in all areas of my life. I think it is a sign of weakness to have addictions. If I can learn to control my stress, I can control my decisions and actions and then be more successful. If I can stop smoking I can do anything is what I believe, which will help my self-esteem. I have been smoking now for 26 years. For each day I don't smoke I think of how much more healthy I can become and how much more positive an image I will have accomplished by quitting. This would be one less thing to be ashamed of. I would be closer to that pure person I am trying to become. After giving up the addiction of smoking I can then quit drinking and then no more partying. I am on a good road to Christianity. I have to learn to trust my gut more and not waiver. I should not have gone out with Barry because he smokes pot. I should have at that point declined the offer of a date and I also should not have gone because I did not have any money and if the date had required it I should have declined.

I am still thinking about the job I passed up and how every month of this year thinking about how my rent will be paid is too stressful for me to continue experiencing. There is a part of me that feels I did the right thing by passing up the job because I really was not up for getting up everyday and putting on a show for people. Also I still have many things to work out for myself before I integrate myself into society. I have a lot of personal issues that need to be sorted out and I need to still work through my stuff with school. I also need to work on my stress level as I continue to tell myself it all works out. I was stressing over Dr. Channing's work and she was out of town. Somehow I think I am always doing the right thing even when I don't know it. But I truly do the best I can. Based on the way a lot of things have worked out I am in a pretty good place to move forward in my life. I need to learn to follow my instincts more.

I worked on my feet today and the funny thing is it didn't hurt like it did the times before. I compare this to—if you work on your stuff regularly enough—it gets easier.

Hopefully, I will get a job on Monday that is the right one for me. Then I can get caught up on my school work and finish this first session of the summer session on time and enjoy Al the man Green next Saturday. I still haven't figured out who I am going to take. God please continue to give me the strength I need to overcome my challenges. Please give me the strength to change the things I can and the wisdom to know the difference.

June 24, 2003

Today is the fifth day I have not smoked. Larry loaned me two hundred dollars to help me out. Now he is in a position where he does not have a place to stay. He has said he is going to get a room at a hotel. When I needed help someone was there for me. I can not call him back tonight because I have had to take care of some things for myself. I did a little exercise, took a shower and as I was taking another step to connect with myself I turned to a NOVA program regarding cigarette smoking. How ironic is it that after 26 years of smoking and trying to now quit, I turn on the TV and there is an educational program on the dangers of smoking. I believe this was all divine. As I took the step to connect with myself God made available to me the something I really needed to help me do it.

After doing all of the things I needed to do for myself, I called Larry. I was relieved to know he has a living arrangement that makes me not have to offer my place. He has a place where he can live for free, but he chooses to stay in a hotel for $80 a day. This means he has options. I am so comfortable with not offering my place and I would be putting myself out. He has the option of a four bedroom house he can stay in for free and alone. I was so surprised he offered to still give me money in spite of his own circumstances. He did ask me about Barry, but I think he is offering to help simply because he cares. He convinced me to stay put for tonight and wait to get the gas from him before driving out to apply for the newspaper job. My horoscope did say to be patient, so I will use this opportunity to get things organized for tomorrow.

My face has been feeling like it is throbbing and my sinuses are draining. But after conducting a thorough search for my guard card and finding it, I seem to feel better than I have felt in days in spite of my not smoking. My energy level actually seems even despite the fact that I exerted so much energy looking for that guard card.

I kind of believe it was healthy to exert that energy and the leveling off might have really come from the accomplishment of the task. Maybe the substitution for the nicotine for me should come in the form of exercise then I'll have more energy for all the things I need to do.

I am concerned about Larry. God please keep him safe and guide him to follow Your wishes.

I have so many people to thank for their support of my school work. When I least expected it, people have been there to support me.

July 23, 2003

My aunt was right. I am too blessed to be stressed. Today I start another adventure. Who knows what this job holds for me. I have taken the time to put together a really snappy outfit with my plaid linen jacket and black linen pants and my suede shoes because I don't know what opportunity is in store for me on this job. I acknowledge the fact that you only get one chance to make a first impression. I'm wondering if this is the mirror experience of how I got into grad. school. As it has been said to me to be nice, I am repeating that to myself that I am nice. I also had a pretty decent cry yesterday when I watched a movie that somehow brought out my feelings about the baby I lost. I found myself patting Buddy while watching the movie as if I was comforting a baby. I did the math in my head and realized at this time is when my baby would have been born or I would have been nine months pregnant. Would it have been some coincidence if the day I held Joy's baby and he went to sleep in my arms is the day I was supposed to give birth to my own baby? I do grieve the loss, but I look forward to the day when my new husband and I will give birth to Faith. Having Faith will change my life and I mean that also in the spiritual sense of the word. My faith has increased and I can feel it in my feet. Somehow I really understand things will always work out. God does work on a need to know basis, therefore, you don't know how He will do it, but He will.

Last Thursday, I filed my final judgment for my divorce and I intentionally wore those pink panties he said he liked. I really do feel myself moving further and further away from him and maybe a part of that is with each month when my body cleanses itself. As I walked across the street to the courthouse to file the papers, I got some sharp pains in my pelvis. My body needs to fully cleanse itself from him. My fear of everything is leaving my body and my faith is increasing. I can remember when I first moved into my apartment and I was afraid to take a shower. Now this is my place and my home and I am now in the midst of exhaling. I am in God's hands and He will take care of me. I also realized my life is aligned in a way that my aunt retired on the day my mother died, 5/1/93 and we are also 30 years apart in age. This all has the significance of the number three and I believe God has lined everything up for me in that when my mother left me my aunt became available. I love you God and please continue to guide me, give me strength and protect me. I love you.

August 6, 2003

I know it has been a while, but here goes. This is that time of the month again. The rent is due. I had a really bad night at work last night. I didn't say anything to anyone. Tonight I have come in and I'm not really in the mood to talk, but I'm doing a little better. Today when I got down on my knees to say a prayer for myself and others—I realized I did ask for the assistance of God, but I really followed it up with thank you. I knew He was going to deliver whatever was being asked, but in His own time. I have learned that He works on a need to know basis. It was at that moment I truly realized the strength of my faith and that I really did believe. I then began my day. I went and turned in my food stamp information so I would qualify for September and promptly returned home to do my work. I made a call to Gerald Harris as he is in a similar situation with his rent. As I am familiar with this process by now, I shared information with him I thought might help him. I also shared with him my lesson of learning to ask for help. He is 32 and is maybe not ready to learn that lesson. I even tried to put it to him in as graceful a way as I could so he would hear it, but I don't think he did. At that point I knew I had done God's work and delivered the message.

We got off the phone with him needing to take a nap. At that time I called Second Chance as the spirit led me to do. This agency is not known for anything but manual labor. The woman I spoke to on the phone was really nice and asked me if I had clerical skills. I said yes. She said that was good because she had an assignment she needed to fill and the young lady she usually works with was not returning her calls. She also said she would be leaving in a couple of hours. I called my aunt and talked to her and she made me laugh so hard. She told me about the new conditions of their trip next month. Uncle Stan said the church people and everyone should have their own music because the church people would play the music so loud it got on his nerves. My aunt also told me the music would be loud and they would be shouting over it in order to be heard. My aunt advised me to go ahead on down to Second Chance even though I was trying to stay home and catch my three day notice that was going to be posted on my door.

I went down there and completed the paper work that didn't even ask me about specific information regarding my past employment. The woman talked with the client. I went to the job site, interviewed with the client and will start tomorrow. The Second Chance situation was all perfect. I could have very well not gotten any information about this position. And the person who would not return Nancy's calls—it was a blessing. I was very restrained in the interview with the Doctor's Hospital employee. Oh yeah, one thing Nancy said to me is, "You won't have to go to Oakland." God is definitely busy in my life.

The Doctor's Hospital employee grated my nerves. It seemed more like she was trying to find a reason to not have me there, but I made it through. In the time I made that call, filled out the paperwork, interviewed and got the job that I will be paid for daily—Gerald Harris had only been sitting at home stewing about his problems. I shared my information with him for the purpose of letting him know it is to be done. Also there is a place where you can get paid in cash the same day you work. He was not enthused for me and his response was, "I knew it was something like that out there." God knows I have done my part to try and help him. Maybe he will just have to learn his lesson the hard way. God only knows.

Talking to him is like talking to a brick wall sometimes. His understanding is so limited. And most of all—just like Douglas said, "People will try to bring you down to their level if they have a problem with you." Gerald definitely has a problem with me, my strength, my knowledge and in his mind in order for him to be the man he thinks he should be, he should be the things I am. He resents me for it. He is a classic example of an insecure man. He could not even allow himself to say he needed to keep his cell phone connected because he needed to be able to reach other people. He said he needed the phone because people needed to reach him. Never hang out with an insecure man. It can be dangerous.

My blessings will come and I am getting my lessons so I can move on through life.

I have also learned about that work thing. The one that seems friendly and probably is—still do not divulge too much information to her. Don't trust her too much either. Don't tell her anything you wouldn't want anyone else to know.

I have just gotten home from work at The Daily News. I think Danny and I have made up. I talked with him about my interest in the Christmas Carol. The auditions are on September 13th. He helped me to understand it may not be as stressful as I thought. I could get a part other than the lead which would mean not many scenes and not much work. The word he used was manageable. I then came home and saw the last few minutes of Any Day Now. The African-American character—Renee, is an attorney running for district attorney. She made a speech to her campaign manager about her needing to run her campaign the way she runs her life, with integrity and honesty. She later won a controversial case and the campaign manager came back wanting to work for her and convinced her he could do the job. The new slogan would be—people over politics. Watching and listening to all of this gave me chills. I can do it.

August 11, 2003

My heart is so full of love for all of the people who are now coming into my life. My heart is also so full of love for God. It seems like things are really falling into place. I fell into this opportunity.

August 12, 2003

Today my aunt and I went to Larry's which is a fruit stand in Fairfield. I was so excited because I thought we were going to pick peaches, but we only bought some instead. We walked around to the different patches and she showed me what all of the different things were. She pointed out to me the zucchini, peach trees, the peas and we even saw two pigs. It was so nice to be out there with her. After we left there we went to Pop's house. He is 89 years old and as aware as I am. When we left I gave him a hug and he said it made him feel better that we came by. Of the peaches my aunt bought me I will make Pop a pie. It is so funny that the pie I never gave to Tony's Papa Bob from the freshly picked peaches he gave me, I will now be able to resolve this with my own grandfather. My aunt was also baking a chocolate cake for Tyrone's youngest son's birthday and she needed some powder sugar for her frosting. She asked me to drive her car to the store. That really made me feel good because it was a definite sign she trusts me. She complains when

Stephen drives her car. I love my life now. It is filled with so many beautiful people and a lot of them are my family. I will have to go by and see Pop and sit out on the porch with him. I want to enjoy life and spend time with him before it is too late. My cousin Stephen is really cool. He took me out for drinks on Sunday and we had fun. I think I am my aunt's favorite niece as she is my favorite aunt. When I get rich she knows I will take care of her like she takes care of everybody else.

August 21, 2003

Right now I'm sitting here at 2:15am at my Daily News job waiting for the garbage man. I told Danny he could leave because he has to be at work earlier than I have to tomorrow. I am trying to be patient, but I must go home because I am very hungry. Danny blurted out to me the memory of a really painful childhood experience. I was so shocked that I did not know what to say. With all of the confusion I have in my life that was a glimmer of hope. He sees me. He thought enough of me to share something so personal. He must really, really like me. That makes me feel so good. I believe Marietta sees me also. We seem to connect. I will try to be patient to find out what God has in store for me as far as a job is concerned. I really like Marietta. She has told her husband about me and she has told me she is proud of me.

The other day I talked with Nancy about spiritual stuff and things I have learned about life. I was so surprised to see the expression of awe on her face. I realized she did not know the things I thought she did. She was really listening to me. After hours of talking to her she asked me when I was going to write a book and I told her it was in the making. She said I needed to hurry up and write it so she could buy a copy for herself and a few others that need it. Over these past few days I have met people that have truly acknowledged my spirit and like me. Marietta even told me she will have to follow my career. I hope that God will continue to bless me with His smiles.

August 24, 2003

I'm sitting here right now waiting to get off of my night job. I had to take stock of some things and realize things always work out and truly how blessed I am. I have been late a couple of times in this past week and it was okay. Tonight I came to work late with my hair wet because I didn't have enough time to dry it. Somehow it worked out. As the night went on my hair seemed to dry very quickly and it was straight so if I still wanted to blow dry it out, it wouldn't be much work. Randy had to leave and pick up Abdul. Frank showed up after he left to do his route. It worked out. There was another person out that was due to return tonight and he showed up as well, so we could all go home tonight.

I believe for me personally things always work out at the last minute or just in time. Tonight I will pray for God to ease my heart and know He will deliver me to wherever He knows I am supposed to be. I will also pray that He will lead me to where I am supposed to go.

August 25, 2003

Today I had a great day at work on my daytime job. The woman I had been having a problem with was really nice and helpful. I seem to have the same feeling of comfort there that I have here on my nighttime job with Abdul and the guys. I like it so much because I am able to be myself. It seems as though the people there are able to see me for who I am and it seems to be working. I am meeting people who appreciate me for who I am. I am so happy I have crossed into this place in my life. Today on my day job I met a man who remembered me from the eighties when I was dating Donte'. He also remembered my mother and Boomer her dog. He asked about them both and genuinely seemed saddened by hearing my mother had passed. He said he was glad to see me and that too seemed genuine. I'm sure it was because it seemed as though I am doing okay in life. From what I have heard lots of people during the early days of my Berkeley years are either dead, in jail or on drugs. I guess he was glad for me that I had not gone down that road. It seems as though God is sending me all the help I need. I don't even know if I asked for it or if He heard my heart and just knew what I needed. I am meeting people in my life now who are supportive—people who want to see me happy. My success will really look like the scene from the movie, The Rookie. Dennis Quaid is the character in the movie who finally accomplished his dream to play as a professional baseball player. The students he had coached told him it was his turn now. They posted flyers all over their hometown announcing the game Dennis would play in. These were the same students he had told, if they wanted something more out of life, they needed to work at it. He also mentioned that working hard at playing baseball and doing their best applies to anything else they might want to do in life.

I can remember the feeling and the look in his eyes when he was told he was going to the majors. The look was of disbelief—like I have waited for this all of my life. I so felt and identified with what I saw him feel. I believe that so mirrored the moment of me finally getting to the end of my journey and completing my studies for my doctorate degree. I can so tell this is going to happen because as the book says, you have to see it, taste it, feel it and believe it, in order to achieve it. That is what that movie did for me. It really made it real for me.

It is also funny that I don't mind being a kid. I am meeting people who are older than me and I don't mind being seen as a good kid. After going through what I've been through and realizing I have so much to learn, I concede to listen and learn. What a change for me.

There was a time when I was content to be the person who knew it all. I guess among my peers I still know a lot, but I have seemed to acquire relationships with people who are older than me and I can learn from. It's also okay for me to not be the one who knows it all. These relationships with my elders still give me a sense of value as an individual because you can tell when they are proud of you and when they respect you. It really means something when you receive respect from people who you truly respect. I guess I have come to a place in my life when I am not only the person who can be counted on, but I can count on others.

People now like me for me. A great line from the movie is from Quaid's father when he tells him, it is okay to think about what you want to do until it's time to do what you were made to do. In the movie Quaid thought the father meant he should not continue his career with baseball and move on to something else. When he finished his first major league game is when he realized his father was actually telling him to continue with baseball. I guess for Dennis that was when he figured it out for himself—because he was great.

I know I was meant to be Dr. Shella D. Bridgeman. I am my father's daughter who is strong and my mother's daughter who is strong and my aunt is proud of me. We laughed about me getting tired of receiving three day notices on my door. I guess in some Asian cultures shaming works for discipline. I guess it works for me too.

August 27, 2003

I am really frustrated with my job. Tonight I talked with Abdul about how to get along with people on the job. I talked about me working on tolerance, patience, diplomacy, flexibility and forgiveness. I expressed my concerns about the seriousness of this list. Abdul said it would be a good idea to pray for wisdom and understanding because having the two of those will help with the things on my list. I am concerned about what type of job would best suit me at this time based on my current challenges.

God has talked to me in that I am aware I am supposed to have this part-time job and He will tell me when it is time for me to leave it. I suppose it will be at a time when I am more secure in myself and in my life.

I love my God as He provides me with everything I need. Because He works on a need to know basis I sometimes spend time trying to figure out what is coming next. My God has never failed me. Every time I have ever really needed something it came to me.

At some point during this evening I started feeling anxious about my situation with my work assignment, but after talking to Abdul and hearing that I should honor my commitment—validated what I thought about him because he advised me to do exactly what I had already decided was best.

I have realized the concerns I have on my job now are old problems from the past. These are not things that are the result of the situation I just got out of. Just as I have looked up and the scar under my eye is now gone. The odor my feet carried that was like the scent of a skunk is also gone. It was something to repel people from me and make me less desirable to others. It is like a miracle that I have been working on this problem for so many years and all of a sudden, my feet don't stink anymore.

It looks like I have worked through lots of layers of my abuse because my eye has healed, my feet don't stink and one internal layer will be taken care of with the help of a good feminine hygiene product. This will be the opportunity to cleanse the rest of that beast out of me. Also because my feet don't stink anymore it also gives people the opportunity to get closer to me. Now that people can get closer to me, they can help me, like me, love me, accept me and just be with me. I have now worn shoes all day that I had worn before and my feet stunk to high heaven. I have worn those shoes now with no odor.

I know too this means my energy has changed because I can remember Joy's baby going to sleep in my arms. I think I can now start chipping away at my stuff. I think the challenges I have now have to do with my financial circumstances. The stress sometimes drains me and affects my mood. I noticed today when I made a decision to be flexible with this job and get the work wherever I can, I immediately felt more energy and I wasn't tired. I believe once I get more financial stability I will be better in every aspect.

I have to work on smiling at men and not showing my teeth because I think even they know the difference. A smile without teeth doesn't mean the same thing. A part of why I show my teeth is because I am proud of them. It's interesting that there's a Blues song I was listening to, that mentioned it is improper to show your teeth to a man. Even Harriet told me that, but I didn't really get it.

September 1, 2003

Today I finally emerged from my three day weekend. I first talked to Alexis and was kind of disappointed that she had such a good weekend. All is well with her and school and she is moving through it.

My situation with school is not bad, but I realized I must complete my old work before I can continue and enroll in any classes. I also finally talked with my aunt after leaving her that card and not talking with her for the three day weekend. I could hear the disappointment in her voice because I was not available and my only explanation was that I slept after working both jobs for an entire weekend. I really did need some time to myself to sort through some things—meaning my life. I have school to work through and I need a job.

After working on my daytime job I also understand I have probably been too hard on myself because the feedback I received from Marietta was, I am easy to work with.

I also believe the things I think are problems right now are things only I can work through. This is the real grown up stuff. I must be very sure about what I manifest and create for myself, so I get exactly what I need. Marietta has said I am <u>all that</u> and for that reason I should not settle for anything professionally or personally and I should want equal to myself or more. I think she solidified for me my mother's death in that when she asked, "What was the cause?" and I said I didn't know. She jokingly said, "Was it an overdose?" My response was the response of when you get a jolt—when you hear the truth. That confirms for me it was an overdose, but was it intentional or accidental. My grandmother's response was, "something went wrong." But she was also trying to cover up something.

September 4, 2003

I received another miracle today. Yesterday I did not know where I was going to get my rent from again. But about 5am in the morning I figured out I had miscalculated my plan in how I was going to do my cash advances for my next two Daily News checks. When I realized I was actually going to have the money it was a big relief for me. The next thing I knew I needed to do was deal with my water bill. I called them and they agreed to give me another week to make payment arrangements with them. Let me say that was exactly what I wanted and it was not a problem. I then got off the phone with them and called Second Chance to speak with Nancy to find out if she had a job for me. The one we ended the day with yesterday was digging ditches on a construction site. Sure enough I called her and she said she had been trying to reach me since 5:40 that morning, but I was on the phone. Because PacBell or SBC postponed my features, I could not receive her call until I ended the other one. We recognized the blessing and I had to be at work for 9am that morning. Even though I had decided to do the substitute teaching thing, I still needed work then. I went and worked the assignment as a receptionist/filing girl and did such a good job they asked me back for a few more days. After completing a day's work there I caught two North County employees in the parking lot and asked them questions about the fees and such for substitute teaching. They were very, very nice and helped me to realize the fees were not as much as I thought. They also gave me hope that they could possibly even be waived and repaid after receiving my first check. I ensured the woman, Crystal, I would be there tomorrow morning to talk to her further.

What I am experiencing at this time in my life is that people are seeing me. That will help me when I work with the kids because they will see me as well. I will also have an understanding of how good it feels for someone to appreciate you for who you really are.

September 21, 2003

I am truly mentally exhausted. My patience is short and I am not feeling very tolerant of much stuff. I did what I was supposed to do and when more was asked of me in a disrespectful way I totally ignored it and began to share these thoughts with myself. I am currently dealing with how I am going to handle all of my responsibilities with the job I have now, the job I have in the daytime and the job I have applied for and my school responsibilities—plus have time for myself. I have not even mentioned my financial obligations of owing people as well as my bills. I am also responsible for writing this letter for Foster. I guess I was asked to help because Stephen did loan me the money I very much needed to give to Jacob. He needed the money right away because he had gotten himself involved in a DUI. Because of that, I truly feel responsible for writing this letter. I feel my mother is with me now while I work through these decisions. There is a part of me that knows there is only so much of this I can plan. I need to trust myself and listen to myself to know what I must do for myself. As I wrote that there is a part of me that says I need to make this week my last week on this job because I need to be rested before I start substitute teaching. Therefore I will spend this next week helping them to clean up that big mess they have so I can feel like I have truly made a contribution. On that following Monday which is 9/29, I will give the district my final information and then wait for them to call me. If I want to start school on 10/26 then this is the route I will take. But there is another part of me that makes me want to work there for two weeks instead, so I can pay Lamont some of his money. The third option is to do both. I can also show up for my day job until they call me for a teaching assignment. The other thing I am having to look at is leaving my nighttime job. It limits what I can do in the daytime. Getting off at 1:30 in the morning affects anything I can do in the daytime. This nighttime job is greatly affecting my lack of sleep. If I can somehow manage to work four days a week substitute teaching I will give up my nighttime job. I was only doing the job because I didn't have anything else. If I can make enough money during the day I will give up my night job.

September 22, 2003

I had one of my worst days ever at work today. I think it might have had something to do with the fact that I am ready to move on to something else. Even though I have fears about the teaching thing, I know it will be a good thing for me to do. It's time for me to take the next step in my life toward my future.

There is a part of me that thinks the people on this daytime job look down on me. I was talking with Stephen this evening and expressing to him my anxiety about my debt. He had a positive take on the situation. He said I should look at it in a way that at least the people were there for me when I needed them. And the other side of that would be what I have heard twice from two different people—you will always have money problems. I think I can deal with having bills, but I don't like owing people. I also felt really good talking to Stephen, in that, I felt like he was really sincere about his feelings toward me. He also mentioned that I tend to go back and fourth with my decisions based on my mood. I told him that is true, but it's my way of fully assessing a situation. I don't even really think it is that I second guess myself, but I guess when I think about it my moods do change, so I change with them. This is a part of me monitoring myself and adjusting my decisions accordingly. I guess I'm not afraid to change my mind. In regards to school, it seems as though I have made it back to my original plan to satisfy all of my personal debts before returning to work. This would also give me a chance to complete all of my schoolwork and not be in a rush. I could take care of my debts and homework and start the new year off on the right foot.

September 28, 2003

I am at a very good place in my life. Yesterday I talked on the phone with Harriet all day. In talking with her I believe I have healed a lot inside. I described it to her in a physical sense that I was ready for a physical relationship with a man because I have done a lot of healing inside relating to the female parts of my body. But I realize I was really saying I have healed a lot emotionally.

October 2, 2003

It's funny how the end is the hardest part. I have done so well with writing in my journal and now at the end of the last few pages, I just can't seem to get it done. Today I had to just slow down and be with myself. I felt like I was moving too fast and I had to take the time to connect with my internal self. I then could be aware of what I needed to do next. In doing that and talking with a person I now consider to be my friend—she gave me some great ideas that led me to add something else that comes out to be a great plan for me. I think I have created for myself something that makes me a lot more comfortable with a plan to teach. It's something about being prepared and how that can really give you comfort you could not ever imagine. I feel really comfortable with it now. I am no longer afraid. I am pretty anxious to find out what is going on with my status with grad. school. I will get on my knees tonight and pray to God and ask for His grace in proceeding with my future. Was the journey about being a teacher, a psychologist, or both? On behalf of myself, I ask God to please ensure me that my place in grad. school is going to be okay. In all honesty, I guess I want to continue with grad. school to become a school psychologist, but more importantly, I am concerned about what God has in store for me. This feeling that I have of connectedness with myself was learned from Dr. Washington. She taught me how to feel my energy. She also taught me to know that feeling and to work with myself not against myself. It's kind of like traveling at a speed you're comfortable with. And when I do that things kind of fall into place. Also knowing how to feel your body enough to know when you're not comfortable and then to acknowledge it and figure out why and then to make the appropriate adjustments accordingly.

October 6, 2003

Today I had a heck of a day. I had to hustle and scramble to gather up the money for my rent. I gave them a check yesterday, pretty much believing I would come up with the money. After all this time, meaning that I have had such financial hardships since I've been here, I finally borrowed money from my boss, Abdul. Today I had to call around town to find a place for me to get a cash advance for a two week period. How ironic is it the same place that denied me in Oakland—I found a place in Berkeley with the same name? I was able to use the same check with the same due date and amount I used in Oakland. I think this is because Berkeley has been so good to me and I am done with Oakland. It was a miracle to see this happen. I have been so blessed with my experiences in life. I talked to Carl on the phone today and was very attracted to him. His strong masculine self was very appealing to me as I've been involved with so many weaklings. Something that bothered me is he kind of admitted he would cheat and I think he said he would not admit it if asked. In spite of the attraction to his masculine strength it also made me very uncomfortable. I had to ask myself why. I think after coming out of an abusive situation where he was not strong, but he was aggressive—that kind of makes me uncomfortable. I also feel like with this type of person they can be controlling and domineering/dominating. After having some days to think about my feelings of discomfort, the answer was staring me right in my face. It was Abdul that allowed me to understand I want the strong silent type. This type of person is gentle and kind but also demands respect in a quiet way. And if necessary can stand up and be heard in a definite way. Someone who is willing to meet your needs and listen to your heart and not challenge you as a person. He is the kind of person who is easy to love. He is not selfish. He is giving. He is gentle, kind, sensitive, good humored, insightful, good natured and intelligent.

October 7, 2003

I realize I am probably depressed. Last night when I got off work I went home and cried. I attribute this to my pinned up fears about life. I think I am being honest with myself when I say it was about death. I have a very strong relationship with death as it has really impacted my life. Both of my parents are gone. I have also lost close friends and co-workers. Death has been prevalent in my life and it has been happening so frequently I fear it happening again to someone I love.

October 13, 2003

After weeks of depression, I have finally come out of my funk. My process was that of a lot of time by myself and a little with others. After a period of time of doing as much nothing as I could manage, I pulled out of it after about two weeks. I guess the doing nothing part is the clearing of the head part, so the next steps can be taken to plan a strategy for life's problems. I feel a lot better right now so I can attempt to make some progress. I also find that as I move through my stuff, I am becoming more confident. I feel more comfortable with speaking my mind and not caring about what anybody thinks. I don't mean in an offensive way or insensitive way. I am becoming more comfortable with myself and beliefs and knowing there's nothing wrong with them and I am entitled to have a difference of opinion with anyone. I have also noticed my depression was self inflicted. I am getting better at blocking out other people's energy. Usually I would get really disturbed by Randy's negative self, but recently I haven't. Also in my comfort with myself I have been more comfortable with racial issues and being a Black woman. I am even comfortable with saying I am a Black woman out loud.

October 23, 2003

My aunt is the one that holds us all together. I question now the quality of her health. She has been having many doctor appointments. She has travelled to Ontario and come back and had a doctor's appointment. She said she thought it was an overactive thyroid problem or a goiter. But today she had a biopsy done on this lump on her throat. Is this lump what causes the cough she has?

I am currently at work on my night job and am trying to refrain from thinking too much about things in a way that I might get overly emotional. Because I don't want to lose control of myself. I did talk with my boss and I shared some things with him and how I feel about them. I mentioned it is important for me to get very busy with putting my life in order to develop my constitution—so I can continue with getting my life on track. I also believe this is important, so if any unexpected life stuff comes up, my life will be on its best possible course. My aunt is so great. This Saturday she is baking two cakes. One is for Foster and the other is for Darren as they are having a combined birthday party in Trinidad. Auntie is not going to make it to the party, but she is going to send the cakes.

October 26, 2003

Yesterday I had a really long day. It started off by me being rushed to get ready for the circus. I was going with my aunt and I was really appreciative of the fact that she was taking me, but I was left with very little time to run my necessary errands. I also wasn't sure of what to wear as we were supposed to go to Orlando afterwards. I was not much interested in going to Orlando to my cousin's house. We made it to the circus forty minutes early which means we could have left later and I could have run my errands. Or if we had done so—we could have probably not gotten such a good parking space. I sat between my aunt and her closest girlfriend. This was a group of church people I was sitting with, which made me feel uncomfortable because the music was contemporary. It was also terribly hot inside the circus. I was worried my ninety-nine cent deodorant would not hold up as I was sweating so profusely. I was hoping to not have another incident like the one I had on Friday on my P.E. teaching assignment where I was smelling something that I came to find out was me.

I am sitting here now writing in my journal as this job is really getting on my nerves. Since last week when my boss was not in a good mood and I left his office, I have kind of not had a place to be while at work. Therefore I have loud TV's blasting in my ears. I have tried to deal with this by putting on headphones and listening to my walkman. I'm not sure if this is working because now I'm just hearing all three. I lately have been coming here in a decent mood, but this place seems to be bugging me. Has my time run out or is it just because I'm tired? Regardless of the reason, I will be glad when I can work one job during the day so I don't have to leave the house at night and I can get a full night's sleep in my bed. I am hoping I can have things worked out for myself by the time school starts on January 26, 2004. Maybe the shift in things on this job has put me in a place where I should be focusing on my homework now. This I think is another challenge for me to work on maintaining my energy. As the challenge presents itself for me when I am teaching my classes, I believe aerobics will help me as a stress reliever, but I probably need to work the yoga in there too because it does help with staying focused.

Once I have taken the time to get connected with myself at work I will understand actually how lucky I am to have this time to myself. Tonight before coming to work I had to deal with the dilemma of having to do something for someone else. I know myself as a very giving person, but I think maybe I had been doing that with my own conditions. This is how I have been able to turn my phone off whenever I needed to. I would like to maintain my sense of self but be able to still give to my family. I am coming to understand they are the most important people to me. I do everything I can to get my rent paid, but I know in my heart as long as that house stands there and it's my aunts, I will always have a place to live. I for the first time in my life have a safety net. But I do admit it's hard to be reciprocal of the love I receive, as I have lots of things my time is obligated to. I have family members that need a job, have kids going to college, are sick, need money, need yard work done, need someone to talk to, need someone to take a long drive with them, need someone to put out their Christmas ornaments, and also some that love me and just want me around. I have for the first time in my life people who truly function as my family. If there is ever anything they can do to help me, they will. There is a part of me that is glad my aunt is leaving until next year, so maybe when she comes back I'll be more established and have one job that pays my bills. Then I'll be working only one job and going to school. I think that's what I've come up with—is one day a week I can stop by my aunt's house. For right now I think it will be on Fridays. This way I will have the weekends to myself. I think I will need this because I will actually only have one day off a week.

I need to also do better with my attendance at The Daily News. I need to make sure I am here at 10pm sharp.

I believe the last of him is energetically leaving my body. This month I started my lady stuff kind of suddenly and I even had really bad cramps as I never had them before. The pain was the same as when the baby was in me trying to come out. I also had the same pains the day I filed my final divorce papers. As I write this all down I realize these are all times when he was being exited from my life physically. As Dr. Washington says, everything that is done positively in the physical world manifests itself spiritually. In the physical world I am growing by leaps and bounds as I have decided to cut my hair off. This will be a very powerful act to release a lot of bad and old energy that is trapped in my hair.

October 27, 2003

I just had a moment tonight at work where I found out the reason why my co-worker left without saying good night last night is because someone did not show up for work. This brings it back to me that when something happens, I take it personally. Meaning, I assume it is me. This is the same as when the program director from school did not call me back and I automatically assumed the worst and I was out of the program—all bad things. The reason for her not calling me back was because she said she had lost my phone number. Now I will have to admit this was pretty irresponsible of her because she could have gotten my number from someone else if she was more conscientious about her work. Also today I had this big deal about not wanting to call the IRS. I was afraid I was going to have to make payment arrangements with them and my funds are already going toward other bills. I talked to them and was informed I am not even in collection status. This means I don't even have to pay any money now and they will just take whatever I owe them from my refund I will get next year.

I am getting to the point now that I don't even want to talk to anyone on this job because I don't want to be here. I am tired of leaving my house at night to come here. I am glad I have the opportunity to earn this money as I still need it, but I am ready to have something more substantial in the daytime so I don't have to come here. This job is in very close quarters and I have to work to find my own mental space. Not that I should let this affect me, but the people here are not in the same place in their lives that I am. I am pursuing good mental and physical health.

I have to ignore the people that don't have good mental health or physical health. I don't want to be in the habit of eating for comfort not hunger. I also want to have good mental health and to be kind enough to myself that I take care of myself. That means eating properly, getting my proper rest and acknowledging my own needs.

I was afraid to call my aunt's house this evening because I didn't want to talk to my cousin and be asked if I have done things I know I haven't had a chance to get to. I have my own mental schedule for when, where, and how I do things. I like to make my own decisions and not be influenced by anyone else. I also don't really think very many people are qualified to speak on the subject of my life as I am a very thoughtful person. Meaning, I take lots of time to think about things before I make a decision. I have also found my timing is something I can feel. I am led and directed to do certain things in my life. My challenge now is understanding how to continue on with my journey in secrecy. Just as I thought it, it came to me. Instead of looking for approval from others and telling them my plans, I will talk to them more about themselves so I won't have to divulge the details of my plans to them.

Harriet is one person I know really understands me because we work with the similar style of manifestation and energy. We both believe you can create what you want and you can banish what you don't want. I feel this way of thinking is essential for the level of which a person can understand me. My aunt, as dear and sweet as she is, mentioned to me a plan B or a what if it doesn't work plan. My teachings allow me to believe what I want—I can have. As Barbra Streisand calls it—desire. I watched Oprah one night and Ms. Streisand told the story of how on a particular occasion there were some flowers (mums) given to her that she sat out on the terrace of her hotel room because she didn't like the color. She has a very specific thing about design and how the colors outside the room should match what is inside the room. Well these flowers did not so as she was displeased. She closed the drapes to the terrace so she didn't have to see them. I can't remember exactly how the story went, but somehow she later became aware that the colors of the flowers had changed to the colors she desired.

This I understood because I have definitely created things myself based on what I desire. This is why I try to be in contact with what it is I really and truly desire. As the book says, I also want to shape my manifestations into things that are fulfilling to me. As a part of the Barbra story I believe she is truly happy with her husband, but I'm not sure when she asked for him she wanted him to be her senior. I don't think she was specific enough. So the other part of that is to be happy when you get it. But try to be specific so you get exactly what you want. That brings to mind the story of a couple I saw on PBS. They were truly in love. The man was totally amazing as a poet, writer, musician and artist, but he was maybe thirty years his wife's senior.

I have talked with myself lately and I am realizing I will be Dr. Bridgeman. But I think I need to be clear that I will also be very knowledgeable in my field. I don't just want the title. I also want the knowledge.

October 30, 2003

Today I was blessed enough to have given a little boy in a wheelchair a drink of water. I think I'll be a good mother because I seemed to have been in tune to what he wanted and needed before I received the cue. Because he could barely speak, I noticed him running his hand across his tray on his chair trying to get crumbs that were left over from the graham crackers I had just given him. I felt so sorry for him. I felt I might as well give him the graham crackers as he might have been suffering in so many other ways. But I did have to finally stop because there was an entire class I might have to deal with that might also want more graham crackers. But in my heart I wanted to give him anything he wanted. When I think of giving a drink of water to the little boy, I think of the conversation Harriet and I had. We talked about being old and in a room alone and hoping there would be someone there to give us a drink of water. I guess when I think about it, today I gave that drink of water to someone.

Children are so beautiful. They can make you appreciate life all over again. Today when I was sitting with Auntie, Oprah was on and they showed a husband giving the gift of a nursery to his wife for their healthy baby that was on its way. He said they had five previous pregnancies and this one the sixth was healthy. He said on national TV how much he loved his wife and she was an inspiration to him. He said all of this and more while crying as if he was about to break down at any minute.

December 1, 2003

Today I have confessed to those closest to me that I am going to have sex with a married man. The two people who did not say anything in objection were Larry and Harriet. Larry didn't address it from a moral stand point. He said to just make sure I don't get hurt. I think Harriet was coming from the same place, but the thing she did caution me about was maybe I might not fall in love, but he might. She also understood my thoughts about not getting married and not having children. My reasons for not wanting to get married were because I don't want to spend the rest of my life trying to please someone or compromising anything to be with them. My life is very full with my family and friends and the career I am currently embarking upon. My heart is currently racing fast as I write this. I think it's because I know there is power in words. Even though I think I've probably told myself I would never be with another married man, today I am a different person and my circumstances and motivations are different. I do not think God wishes me to do this, but I know He still loves me and knows my heart. As I think of this thing I am about to do, I can somehow appreciate people who care enough for me to let me live my life with my own decisions. I think the men might object because they wish it was them and the girlfriends because they wish they could do it. I also believe people put me up on a pedestal as their leader and I am only a human being. God will lead me to where I need to go. Not those with their own opinions about me.

I have doubts about having children because I am supposed to help many and I am not sure what I would have left after giving so much to the rest of the world and so many other children. If I had children I would want to be there for them and if I was married I would want to do that a certain way also. I just question how all of that fits into the plan that God has for me. Within the next couple of days I am going to have sex with this man in order to get that crazy energy from my marriage out of me. I am also going to cut my hair off to start anew before the new year gets here. I am really feeling impatient about my transition. As I think right now where I am with myself, it's right on time for my boss to not be at work so I can spend this important time with myself.

January 12, 2004

Well, I have finally made it to this day. I have to complete the last few pages of this journal I received almost a year ago. I at least can say I have come a long way. This time last year I was a mess. I was timid and afraid and I believe my external wounds have healed and the internal stuff has definitely progressed. I am on the verge of finding out for the last time if they are going to let me stay in school. I guess I can remember all of the times they have worked with me and let me stay in. They have given me option upon option and I have not taken advantage of any of the chances they have given me. But now I am ready. I have the jobs, the experience and the courage to face whatever might come my way. I can truly understand everything that was said to me today in relation to what reason do they have to allow me to continue. I have been given the option to write a letter which will convince them they have reason to offer this to me. I am prepared to accept anything that comes my way in relation to the outcome of this last go round with these people. I must trust in God and I believe in His will and I am prepared to follow His choices for me. He has never failed me. At the darkest times of my life He was preparing me for something great. I went from this time last year to now being a productive member of my community. People know me and like me in the city of Berkeley. I am not sure what God has in store for me, but I know it will be in Berkeley with the support of my friends and family.

January 15, 2004

I finally feel like I am making progress in my life. I am working with the special kids and it feels great. I have learned they have so much to offer. I have learned they are so appreciative of anyone who cares about them. They are also very sensitive to the feelings of others. This means they are perceptive of my moods. They can feel my moods. This makes me accountable for my emotional state so it does not affect others in a negative way. I think working with them also gives me the opportunity to do the work I want to do with students. My time with these students gives me a chance to do counseling. I love these kids. Working on this job, I am in a supportive environment and I think that is what is important. I'm so happy things are starting to look like the life I visualized. When I go to work at night I look the way I had envisioned I wanted to look. I look presentable and comfortable. I would not have to be embarrassed if I saw anyone I knew. My whole life is looking like the life I envisioned for myself.

February 1, 2004

This is almost one year to the date when I started this journal. I have had many occurrences in my life since then. My most recent events have put me to the challenge to find out just how far I've come. I've cut my hair off, corrected my Godparents, gotten divorced, started substitute teaching, started school on 1/27, had sex with Troy on 12/22 (mom's birthday), worked on asking for help, worked on giving love, been totally blessed and given a second chance to do what I'm supposed to do. And decided I want to be on the School Board and Mayor of Berkeley.

I realize I must not judge if I don't want to be judged and I must give love if I want to be loved and I must have forgiveness if I want to be forgiven. I have also realized as I heard a woman say on TV, that as long as you have family you feel you can conquer anything. In order to continue to move forward I commit to using my sage for bad energy, reciting a daily mantra to empower myself and stop judging others as I don't want to be judged myself. I will also give love so I can receive love.

November 11, 2004

I am in a really good place with myself today and at this time in my life. I have learned so many things from people around me and from my own life experiences. I feel so alive. I currently want to jump up and down with excitement because I am so sure I am where I am supposed to be today. I have made all of the decisions I was supposed to make and I have picked up on all of the cues, therefore, I am getting the lessons. I am using all of my past experiences and applying them to things that come up today. I can say to myself I am finally getting it. Joyce Meyer has been a big help with this process. One day I looked at one of the shows I had taped a while ago and one of the things she said was, you are beyond asking someone for prayers for you because you should be leading prayers for others. I also appreciate my friend Harriet for not being available. She forced me to stand on my own two feet and rely on my own instincts and draw from my own experiences. We had a conversation one day and I told her my feelings about her being safe and her being out late at night. She told me she understood what my feelings were, but she was going to do what she wanted to do. This made me realize that people can have a lot in common, but ultimately they have to do what is best for them or what they think is right.

Another experience I had was the voting experience for the 2004 presidential election. I voted for Ralph Nader for president because my conscience would not let me vote for John Kerry and his stem cell research. This was prompted by a young man who came on channel 9 before the election and said your vote is like vouching for someone. If you vote for them you are saying you support them—as if you were being used as a reference for someone applying for a job. This made me understand I had to vote according to my principles.

I also understand I must always be true to God no matter what the situation. I also realize if I am true to the principles of God's will then I will be okay.

November 30, 2004

My mother understood I was a lot like her. She realized there were things about her that made her life harder and she didn't want me to suffer in the same way. That is why she always told me, "No man is an island." She lived as an island—on her own. She didn't ask for help and avoided what she thought was drama or confrontation. She would just deal with the problem on her own. An example of this is when Cynthia told me my mother had lived with her and her mother briefly with my two brothers before I was born. This was because my mother would not deal with a woman at social services who had her information wrong. I also remember me and my mother being evicted from a house a woman owned and wanted to sell. We did not find another place to live in time so my mother and I had to live in an abandoned house for a short while. This was because my mother would not reason with the woman to make sure we had a place to stay. Wrapped up in all of this is my mother's strength, but it was also her weakness. No man is an island. You have to deal with other people. Understanding my mother in this way, Bobby does not know what it probably felt like for my mother to finally give him to his father. Acknowledging she could not do it on her own and she needed help was probably really hard for her. She also knew I had my own mind. Just like her. As my grandmother told me, my mother decided to change her own name when she was about sixteen. I am now at a time in my life when I need the lesson of dealing with difficult situations and people. This challenge presented itself to me on a job I have just started on the weekend and it has showed up again with this agency situation. Both of these circumstances were brought to me in a way that they absolutely must be dealt with to help with my well being. This means my lively hood.

January 16, 2007—3:16am

I have to finally let this go. This reminds me of the journal entry Oprah made before the first show she did that started her now famous empire.

I am so nervous. Tomorrow I will return to school with my first official day of teaching of the new year. I have been silent for many days at the request of God. I have been trying to reconnect with Him so I can clearly hear His voice. I can say I am getting there, but I'm not totally back to where I was. Something that made me feel good was while watching a program about a man that marched with Dr. King, he mentioned at 88 years of age he has just realized one of the most valuable ways of communicating with God is just by sitting in His presence and listening. This is my main way of communicating with God is by just sitting and listening.

I am so nervous about tomorrow because it is such a big day. God had confirmed to me I have been chosen to do His work and as a part of that I must understand my responsibility. Every word that comes out of my mouth must be pure and true. I must represent Christ well. He has given me the assignment of apologizing to my classes for possibly humiliating them. I have to admit I am afraid and uncomfortable with it. And I must be sincere or else they will know. After finishing the Road Less Travelled as instructed by God, it has been validated for me that the feelings I have of being alone are real. This is a special kind of aloneness that is good but isolating. I have the pleasure of knowing secrets God only shares with me. But they are just that, things I can not share with other people because they wouldn't understand. I feel alone, like it's just me and God. I know I'm not the only one. I just don't know anymore.

January 19, 2007—2:09am

Today I had a very interesting situation. It was Thursday night at the church. This is the night for the Middle School Youth Group to meet. Last week I met the youth pastor and we talked about his vision for the future with the youth of the church.

After that happened I felt really stressed about what God wanted me to do. I had been so disconnected from God I have been working on getting back to where I was—obedient and hearing Him. I listened to all of my Joyce programs and I've been reading my love devotional as well as my Joyce devotional and I'm still unsure.

I do feel myself connecting to God, but I don't know if He wants me to help with the youth, or if He wants me to join a group in church. I do believe during last Sunday's service the pastor looked at me when he said, "You can't learn to love by being in a room by yourself."

Tonight I was really tired but had really felt God wanted me to go to the youth meeting tonight just to show the kids I love them, but I lay down to rest for a bit and didn't get up.

One part of the reason why I didn't want to go was because I was tired. But the other part was because I would have been outing myself. The kids would have obviously known I was there because I wanted to be around them and the pastor would have known who I was and talked to me. I am afraid of the responsibility. And I'm telling myself I'm not sure about what God wants me to do. I am afraid to really be seen because I have been used to being in the dark for so long.

January 25, 2007—1:07am

Tonight was the second night I attended the church to support the kids. I felt a little weird and annoyed because one of the pastors asked me who I was. I wasn't really in a good mood. I was tired and didn't really want to be there, but I will do anything God asks me to.

I sat and watched the kids and had some laughs, but I still felt kind of weird, like obvious. I am aware I am to attend because someone needs to see me there. But it still feels a little weird.

I also noticed the African-American males really need a presence of an African-American role model. Where are the brothers? As much as I wanted to and probably needed to, I could not stand up when the pastor asked if there was anyone who wanted to be nicer. I just couldn't do it.

After getting home I felt kind of sad like something was missing and I still don't know what that was. I don't know if it has something to do with this project I am still trying to hammer out at work. Because I just feel lonely and sad.

I really like Ms. James and I think she's a nice person, but I pray that she finds her way to God's plans for her life.

January 26, 2007—1:44am

God gave me a gift today. While I was standing in line at Super Foods, I heard an African-American male speak to someone on the phone about making God first in your life. I felt this was a gift because I was just mentioning the necessity of African-American involvement with Christ. Also last night after church with the kids I felt empty like something was missing. But when I got to school today my most quiet and shy student spoke up during the middle of class about why she couldn't do her homework. It was because she was at church. She also readily joined a group when I asked her to and that has usually been a problem. I am happy to have gotten a response to my efforts so quickly. She also asked me if I was going to be there every week. She said she didn't want me to, but her actions in class showed that because I was there she was more outgoing and productive. God has also shown me that it doesn't have to be an African-American male, but just an African-American makes a difference.

I want to acknowledge I know for sure God has chosen me. I watched two programs this evening and God spoke to me through the both of them. God has told me He has chosen me as a prophet and I must lead and teach His people. It was clearly stated to continue teaching. Because if you teach them maybe they will save themselves. I also know now sometimes how you are led to that understanding is not pleasant, but it doesn't make it any less true. I feel peace in knowing for sure God has chosen me to build the bridge to Him.

Today God has informed me of why I haven't had my financial windfall yet. It's because He wants me to become a better steward of what I currently have before He gives me more. I do tithe and save ten percent, but He wants me to stop going to the check cashing place as of right now. That probably also falls into the category of you shouldn't be doing things you are ashamed of and I am definitely ashamed of that. I do love the

Lord for being in my life and standing by me.

February 21, 2007—11:56pm

What I know for sure is the more time you spend with God—the better off you are. Last week or so when I was having the trouble on my job, I would stay up late nodding at the computer listening to my Joyce Meyer programs. Even though I was totally exhausted and not getting more than 4 hours of sleep each night, I had my most successful days at work during that time. I sat with the vice principal and was able to communicate my issues to her while remaining calm and collected. I can even remember having an extremely calm day when students had really tried to push my buttons.

I pray to God that I will soon be better than I am now. I want to be patient, kind and loving on a daily basis. As Joyce says, I am going to have to find my formula.

My lesson is also that you can not be humble until you are confident. Humility is one of the greatest tools to have in your arsenal. It is very disarming and helps you to remember that you don't know everything. And if you don't know everything you won't think yourself better than others. And you might be kinder, then people might be kinder to you. I truly in my heart of hearts want to be the best servant of God ever. I now believe God has told me I just need to be grateful for the baby I am going to receive whether it be a boy or a girl.

February 22, 2007—1:08am

I have learned today for sure the devil is busy and real. I stressed today over attending the Thursday night service at the church. I had imagined in my mind they were going to ask me to do something to help them out and lo and behold it was one of the greatest nights ever.

Alejandra preached and she was fantastic. She was moving and relevant and genuine. I could not wait to congratulate her after she finished with the spectacular message she preached on anger.

I know the kids felt it just like I did.

I was also able to share with her about how much I hated coming there on Thursday nights and I was mad at God for making me do something that was so uncomfortable for me. But I can see now I have to be patient and God will work it out.

Today twice I have gotten the message about letting go of a relationship that is not working, so I know God is trying to tell me something. I wonder who it is.

February 28, 2007—12:04am

Lord please tell me what this is here to teach me. I keep having the same situation with the needy kids. We seem to have a stand-off regarding love. They try to get more from me than others do. As a result, they end up getting mad at me because I refuse to give in.

There is some part of me that actually resents them asking for more than I am offering. I feel like they would be taking something away from me. I only have so much to give and it is also rude to demand more than others.

Do I understand they probably need it? Yes. But I also believe a more proper way to fill ourselves up is to love ourselves. But aren't those people something like leaches. In that they want to suck you dry. Those types of people can never be satisfied and they are willing to do anything to get it.

I was trying to compare this to people asking me for things and it really getting me upset. I think the difference is these kids usually are willing to do anything to get love and that can be dangerous. They demand it and if they don't get it there is usually trouble. And if you give it to them no amount is ever enough to fill that hole only God can fill.

Is the lesson in all of this to recognize a kid that has problems and run for the hills? The needy kid must go because if they don't get what they want they can be trouble.

Also I realize this has never ended in a good way because it's really a chess game. They make the move to try to force my love and I don't give and that makes them show their hand—making it clear to me what they really want.

The lesson is, I have seen this enough times to know where it is going. So use wisdom and get them moved ASAP.

The devil sure does stay busy. He had me going through all of that drama in my head this past weekend about my brother and his family coming over and they already had plans.

March 16, 2007—10:26pm

I realize You have now given me the desire to have someone in my life. I have met people and for one reason or another we will probably not have a close relationship. But I do recognize You are now allowing me to have a desire for others in my life.

Deal breakers are jealousy and competitiveness. I believe those are things that are not healthy. I wonder where God is going to lead me. It's getting pretty interesting. I have recovered my relationship with God and He is giving me more confidence to let me know no matter what happens—He is going to take care of me.

I keep getting the message it is time for me to tell my story. I have noticed I do feel less shame when I tell it. I also find it liberating and I don't care what people think. This is only because God is growing me to know what is important. I am so looking forward to all of the things God is going to bring into my life.

Is it $100,000 that is going to come my way? And God is saying to make sure not to give it away. And is He also saying the school He wants me to start is in my home? I know God is doing fabulous things in my life so we'll just have to wait and see. And is the baby coming in April?

March 20, 2007—3:20am

I have noticed the perfectly timed hand of God working in my life. On this day, Joel was talking about divine connections and I can feel it happening in my life.

Tonight I caught up on Joyce's show and at some point I was crying because God was telling me to get out of the boat and walk more in faith. He told me a lot of things He's going to ask me to do are going to be uncomfortable and new, but I should do them anyway. I know specifically I am now led to share my testimony about my life with God. With the power of God inside of me I will succeed at whatever He has called me to do. This is just like the talk I gave at Cissy's father's service. It was like what Joyce said about her first time speaking to an audience. My mouth got dry and my lips stuck to my plastic braces and my heart was beating so loudly I was afraid everyone could hear it through the microphone. I followed the Holy Spirit to say what I was led to say and people were truly moved. Carrie was practically in tears and many people congratulated me on what I had written. The Spirit must have really shown through my work because one woman asked me what church I attended. I say all of that to say you never know how the Lord is going to use you if you are willing to follow His will.

I feel that turning point coming in my life where God is taking me to another level of service. I have to be truly willing to trust Him and get out of the boat. God has put it on my heart to write my testimony to make sure what I need to say is said. For God I will do anything.

March 22, 2007—6:49pm

I must continue to listen to God and follow His lead as to who I need to talk to and share my vision or His plans for me. I'm sure it will all come together.

It is very crucial that I spend a lot of time with God right now so I can continue to hear His voice. God loves me and He wants the best for me. So I have to continue to trust in Him and lean not on my own understanding and He will make my path straight.

April 8, 2007—3:15pm

I almost didn't make it to church today, but God's little angel led the way. This was one of those days when I was so tired I thought I was going to lose my mind. I thought it would be too dangerous for me to even drive around the corner to church.

Last week was the first Sunday I had the baby and so of course we went to church. Now that I think about it, that prayer Pastor William put on the baby might have helped me already. This Sunday even though it was Easter I believed God would forgive me for not attending church due to my condition. This morning the baby was having a hard time and I was shooting for the 9:30am service, but we couldn't make it. As time went on I just thought it wasn't for me to do. Then the baby woke up fussing and I didn't know why, but it was just enough time for me to take a shower, get dressed and get to the 11:00am service. After I got dressed I gave the baby a little more milk and then was ready to go. He even cooperated while I put him in his car seat. After we did all of that, he looked at me with his eyes wide open as to say, mommy I know what I did and I want to go to church today. This little boy is really special because after all of that I knew there was a special reason for me going to church today.

I was very late, but there was the perfect seat left for me and the baby to sit in front next to the videographer. And because we were so late and it was Easter Sunday, practically the whole church saw us walk in. This I believe was to our advantage because at the end of the service Corrie came over and talked to me about some things. It turns out she is very much in transition also and wants to do some Christian based work. I asked her what did she want to do and she said she would follow my lead because I am obedient. This takes me back to Moses last night on TV. It was said that the people were looking for someone to follow. God chose Moses for the people to follow out of bondage, but he had to wait on God to lead him. All God told him was to gather the people. He had to stay connected to God the entire way in order to know exactly what to do.

It also came to me that—you dare not question God when you

have seen His work. Also, He has kept His promises. God's promises were also the topic of Easter Sunday's sermon. God has kept all of His promises to me. So I need to just follow what He asks me to do. But I need to stay connected so I know what He is saying to me.

Moses also claimed himself to be a prophet. God has chosen me to share His Word so people can know His works and get to know Him.

April 13, 2007—Friday—10:47pm

My God, I made it through this day. Today was the six month time line I needed to wait to find out if I have H.I.V.... Whew!! I don't have it. Boy, I won't do that again. I also finally caught up on some of my time with God. This means as of this morning I finished watching at least 2 week's worth of Joyce. This is a main stay in my spiritual walk with God.

Before resuming my time with Joyce, I realized my jealousy and bad words against Pastor John were working against me. I repented and asked God to forgive me. Then I felt better. Joyce's program addressed exactly what I had done and how it can block up your well, so to speak. Joyce also confirmed when you are feeling a bit off it's better to be quiet. I do realize I need to recommit to not complaining and not saying bad things about others.

After all of that, watching the last program that aired on 4/13 talked about if God has asked you to give up your full-time job and go into ministry it is possible, but God would have to do certain things. He would have to provide a certain type of assistance. There would have to be some type of flow and it would be a good idea to move slowly to be sure you have gotten this request from God. Joyce gave an example of when she first started. A woman was led by God to give her free childcare and then later when she did pay her it was only $50 per month.

God knows I have this child to take care of so I definitely need money. I do believe I have a close enough relationship with God to know when He is talking to me. I do know for right now He has told me to free up that energy of bad I had cast on myself by speaking ill of others and being jealous. You will never get what you want by not wishing others well.

I also know I need to hurry up and energetically disconnect from that school so other things can come to me. An example of this is the day I told the principal I needed to leave. The next day I got a call for a child. On the day I actually committed to leaving is when the call came to pick up first a little girl then Walter. During the time he was conceived is when God had put it on my heart to sign up to be a foster parent. God did tell me the child that came to me would be the child that was supposed to be with me and he would be adoptable. But I thought it was odd because He told me to go through this foster care agency.

Monday, Walter and I are going to court to possibly meet his birth mother and grandmother. The questions I want to ask if possible are, where does the name Walter come from and how is the last name pronounced?

April 15, 2007—Sunday—6:41am

I am up at this hour because I have been up all night. God directly told me to finish those papers for my teaching job. I physically almost got sick while doing them. I guess that is a sure sign I needed to leave. After I finished the papers, I moved on to do some other things I needed to do like cook some food for Sunday and get ready for church. I even got the baby's stuff ready also.

While completing all of these tasks, I had a chance to do some thinking. I don't know why, but God wants me to totally disconnect from that school and maybe even the school district. Yes, I believe it's the school district also. I need to become invisible to them and disappear. God is telling me before I can open another door I need to close this one first. That is why I need to get my things from that room in the school. Because people are too curious and all they want to do is ask questions. I need to be done with that school and not return. And because of this God is telling me to not have the small group. I need to slow down and focus on this little baby God has given me to take care of and listen to His next instructions. It is very clear to understand caution should be used before starting a new venture.

April 15, 2007—Sunday—10:06pm

How freeing it is to finally be finished with that job. The pastor asked today in the service who are you? I know I am a child of God and as a child of God I must have an occupation that reflects that. I know I'm going in the right direction because he mentioned Moses leading the people. This is the connection I have made before about what God is asking me to do. The pastor said that Moses gave up everything to serve God and that is exactly what I have done. That is the reason why God chose him because he was ready to follow Him with a committed heart. God knows I will do anything for Him. I am also led to meditate on this for the week. But on Sunday I'll ask the pastor about his plans for a school. And let him know God has instructed me to start a school also and that I have left my job and need employment by the fall.

April 16, 2007—Monday—4:51pm

This level of pain is unimaginable. The baby left today. I really loved him. I didn't think it was possible to have such pure love for a person. This morning he lay on my chest and spit up on me and I didn't care. All I wanted was for him to be happy.

All I keep thinking is, God will use this for good and lean not on my own understanding. There is a part of me that makes me think I am still only saying goodbye to people. I do think we should value each other more because we don't know when anyone will leave us. If I had known today was my last day with him, I would have loved him more. I would have held him and kissed him and told him I loved him. When I think about it I do believe I did all of those things. I think I just would have paid more attention.

I do know this was supposed to happen because everything was timed perfectly. He was exceptionally good this morning even while I went to my job to drop off the last of things. It was as if he knew our time together was ending. He allowed me to complete my laundry, get dressed and give him a bath. After I bathed him and dressed him he lay on the bed quietly while I got dressed. This was beyond unusual. I was running a little behind and he got into the car seat with no trouble. This was way too unusual. We drove to Oakland and got a great parking space and then had to go through security. He didn't make a peep while I took him out and it happened quickly. Just as I arrived on the second floor a woman looked at me and they were at that time about to call in the baby's case.

After that it was all shock and confusion. It had been decided by the social worker the baby would go home with his birth mother and her foster mother. Things were so perfectly timed that the social worker was available. We all know how possible it was for him to not be at his desk to receive the call or to be out of the office. Otherwise, they were thinking of putting this off at least until tomorrow. The social worker showed up and that was what they needed in order for the baby to go. I wrapped him in a blue blanket and gave him to his birth mother's foster mother. I also gave her the two extra diapers I had along with the pacifier and formula and bottle. He was wearing a yellow onesie and yellow booties.

When she took him she said to him he has gotten so big. Then she handed him to his birth mother and she looked at him like he was a stranger. The foster mother stood up and hugged me and I did not embrace her back. She thanked me for taking such good care of the baby and said she used to be a foster parent also. I looked at her very strangely and made her aware that when she hugged me I got lipstick on the jacket of her white linen suit.

The birth mother's White male attorney was talking to me introducing himself and I looked at him in a strange way.

When it was over I coolly dismissed myself and strolled down the hall to the elevator, all in the plain view of everyone. I very coolly carried away my empty car seat that in my heart belonged to a baby I left with strangers. When I got downstairs and went past the security guards that had delayed me coming in, I walked quietly past them and intentionally didn't make much eye contact. I didn't want them to realize the carrier was now empty. I didn't want to feel embarrassed because they probably felt from my energy I really cared about the baby and he was mine.

As I walked down the street with the empty carrier I felt ashamed and hoped no one knew it was empty and they did not know the baby was just taken away from me. I struggled for the past three weeks carrying that carrier and now I longed for that extra weight.

I held my head up very high as I walked down the street to my car so no one would know what I was suffering through. I wanted to call the agency, but I could not let out any signs of pain or weakness. I held it in and drove and when I got to Berkeley I called the office and Madea asked if I was okay. I said yes of course and that I didn't need to talk. Before I got to Berkeley I stopped in Fremont to check my mail. There was a key indicating I had a special package. It was a package regarding the baby's medical insurance. My thoughts were to take everything to the office to get it out of my house and possession. But by the time I got home all I wanted to do was to be with him. That made me look around to see what would remind me of him. For some reason I was able to get everything pretty much in order before I left so things were pretty tame. In the kitchen were prepared bottles all lined up and the one bottle he had used before we left and his last bottle. His yellow bath towel lay on the hamper and his two wash clothes hung in the bathroom. At this point I just wanted to grab anything that still had his smell.

The little sour smell of the formula he drank was in all of the clothes in the hamper. I smelled the items and remembered him clearly. I went to the computer to look at the picture Stephen had sent me and to send out the e-mail to friends to recount this morning's e-mail announcing the baby. The message only said the baby went home to his birth mother. This was only on the subject line and nothing in the body. It was almost like I was announcing a death.

I sat on my bed and looked at my special place in my room and there I saw the baby's birth card with his foot prints. He left his foot prints behind. He made an impression on me. That tiny person had so much strength, physically and mentally. His first week, he could hold the pacifier in his mouth. The second week he could hold his own bottle and just today he almost jumped out of the tub while I was bathing him. I looked at him kind of crazy and he looked at me with concern like he knew he was risking his safety.

This baby is from God and I think he knew. I remember, I think it was yesterday when he grabbed my finger and looked at me in the eye and said thank you with his eyes. He realized I was doing the best I could to take care of him by unclogging his nose. I also realize he loved me because he would cry just for me and nothing was wrong with him. I believe he loves me too and he will miss me. He will miss lying on my chest to be burped or sleeping in the bed next to me or just my touch and voice.

I will miss his loud burps and poots and checking his diapers for the smell and color. I will miss talking to him about his stinky booty and that I needed to clean it. I will miss his cries of opposition and need. He cried as soon as he awoke to say, I'm hungry. I will miss how he was starting to smile at me and he did it as if he had a secret. I asked him if Ma or Grandma was talking to him and he looked at me like he understood.

I am no longer in the special class of mom. This feels like it felt when I lost my baby this last time—because that baby was real too.

God told me he was mine, but He took him away. I have to believe it is a part of His great plan for my life.

April 17, 2007—Tuesday—3:42pm

Today is better than yesterday. I can't believe I was able to get out of bed, wash my face and brush my teeth. God must be holding me up. God has made it so that the country is grieving the way I am. Yesterday was the day of a 32 person killing at Virginia Tech. Of course while it was happening I didn't really trip. But today I am in mourning like everyone else.

I lie in the bed for most of the day waiting to hear from God. Somehow at 10am I was awakened to Joyce's program. The subject for this week is abuse. Somehow at the end of the program the guest mentions, a baby will die if it is not loved. That it can be given all of the essentials like food and water, but if it is not loved it will die. This made me open my eyes because those were the exact words Terrence said to me yesterday. That let me know the baby could be in danger. Later in the evening when I finally got out of bed, I shed a few tears because I realized I was so weak from not eating. I was dizzy and almost fainted. Also the first thing I saw when I walked out of my room was the baby's last bottle sitting on the kitchen counter. His spirit is still in this house.

I watched the program and mourned with the nation and realized I should take this time to grieve. I watched The View and realized it was okay to not get rid of those clothes that still have the baby's smell. That it's okay to talk about him and that he really was here.

I still lay in my bed and slept and believed I was fasting and waiting on God to tell me the next thing to do. I got up and sent Stephen an e-mail asking how I could get a picture of the baby without looking at the computer and I realized there was an e-mail from Alice. She quoted parts of a Scripture—"Those that are faithful to God He is faithful to them." I am hoping the faithful part means God is going to keep His promise to me about the baby and adoption.

I shed a few tears and still tried to figure out what to do. So I went over and looked at the most recent CD Joyce had sent me. I came to my room and put it in and she said to go to God and ask for what you want boldly. That was the greatest relief I had yet. That was when my appetite came back and I felt like a true burden was lifted off of my chest. It seemed like that was the answer I was looking for. I had to ask for what I wanted and believe with faith I would get it. So that's what I did. I also prayed for the social worker that he would have understanding and wisdom to guide him in seeing to the welfare of this child. I also prayed for favor with anyone who could help to get this child back to me.

Tomorrow I will go to the church to hear a woman's story about her being in foster care and I believe that will reveal something to me. Also I believe it is God's work to have this presentation just after the baby left. This is very convenient, definitely not an accident. I will continue to listen to God and wonder if I am to stop in to see the youth at the church tomorrow or not.

I also wanted to acknowledge that I did not take the baby for granted. When I looked at all of the photos I had taken of him, I realized I did take the time to enjoy him in spite of everything else that was going on. Proof of that is, as busy as I was, on the last day he was here I took at least 3 pictures of him. When I did that I wasn't even thinking he would no longer be here. The other pictures I have of him are a good amount also. They were taken on different days when he was sleeping a certain way or if we had come from a bad day at the doctor. I was a little distracted by my job, but I was truly loving him everyday and I know he knew that. That's why we need to be together. Because I believe we need each other. I believe he is God's promise to me. So I will go on everyday with my heart open, loving him and missing him and waiting for him to come back to me. I will not close my heart to him. My believing he is coming back makes it not hurt as much. It just makes it seem like he's away and God is just getting some things in order. I think I will use my new found humility and call the social worker and the placement person who placed him with me to let them know that if anything happens with the baby to please call me. But the most important thing is to stay connected to God. I wonder if I should talk to Pastor William tomorrow about his vision for the school. I will wait on God to direct me.

April 20, 2007—Friday—8:38pm

I really miss that baby. I feel so alone. I guess I pass that test because I really want what's best for him. Even though I know I could love him and probably give him all of the material things he needs, there would come a time when he's older and he needs to know his birth mother really tried to take care of him. God will take care of him and follow through with whatever plans He has for his life. And because he is such a special little boy I know God has plans for his life.

I heard God say today that I should be expecting a miracle since I've been so obedient to Him. Pretty much it was stated on Joyce's program. Her husband told her that she gave up her job to go into ministry, so she might as well have some fun because God is going to deliver a miracle. This makes me believe the baby is coming back to me, but I still miss him. I must really be stressing because I am having a lot of tension in my head. I did what God said I should do and spoke with Madea and told her I'm available for a baby that needs me. I'm trying to think of someone other than myself. Tonight I watched Grey's Anatomy again and what a difference a day makes. One of the characters on the show had an issue with her daughter she gave up for adoption. What I realize about my own life is it was good for the baby to go to his birth mother because everyone deserves a second chance. This is something really important to look back on someday and regret. I'm glad I can see this is good for someone other than myself. I don't believe I have been able to think so much about someone other than myself, or even look at things from someone else's perspective. This is also what's best for him because he would want to know she at least tried to take care of him. God is definitely doing a work in me. I have increased my forgiveness, sensitivity, compassion, understanding and ability to love.

When I rubbed that ointment on the baby's bottom I knew something was happening to me. Being a parent and loving a child softens your heart and makes you a better person. I have noticed I am not very interested in the children I see while I'm out during my day. I still know children are beautiful and amazing, but I am still grieving the loss of my own. The day he returns to me will be probably the happiest day in my life. I know God is looking out for me.

April 20, 2007—Friday—10:17pm

God is really trying to send a message to me because I turned the TV to channel four and there is yet another program about a parent and a biological child being abandoned. The young man is expressing to his biological father he has heard he was aware of his birth, meaning he was abandoned. I even saw a short on channel 9 entitled Everything Happens for a Reason. A woman's daughter died and custody of the newborn child was denied to her because she wasn't together enough. The worker told her he would revisit the situation in a number of weeks and then make a decision. The movie ended with the woman dressed in business attire and laughing and playing with her grandson and he looked to be about ten years old. This indicated that she got herself together and everything worked out. The man gave her custody because she got herself together and kept herself together. But when I look at it this way, I wonder what is going to happen with me and the baby. But I must trust in God. Like He says, I am going to get a miracle and He's going to work everything out so don't worry. Because everything always works out.

April 21, 2007—Saturday—3:40pm

Today I finally had peace. Last night while I was up fiddling around with that picture for Alexis' birthday, Dr. Gene Scott was on TV talking about God being the light of his life and that no matter what happened God would see you through. The key for me was he gave that Scripture again that said, "You have not because you ask not." This was my exact third time hearing it which meant the baby is coming back to me for sure. All I had to do was ask. Dr. Scott was also saying you should live expecting. That was the exact handout I had on my nightstand from church. The title was Living Expectantly. This means if you have faith in God you will wait and expect certain things to happen in your life.

Today I put action behind my beliefs and talked to the baby in the spirit because this is the time he is usually sleeping. I told him to be good and strong and this is all a part of God's plan. This would give his birth mother a chance to make peace with this situation and this would work to his benefit when he was older. I also told him this would give me time to have more clarity about some things in my life and have more faith in God. I told him God is watching out for him and everything would be okay and he should listen to God when He speaks to him. I told him I know God speaks to him because he often has a look like someone is talking to him when he is looking in another direction. And when he is sleeping and when he is smiling. I know that God spoke to him on the day he left and the days he got us to church. Because he is a child of God. I told him to keep the secret that I love him and let that be one of the things he holds on to while we are apart. I told him to not give the ladies too much trouble because we both know how he can be and they are doing the best they can.

I told him I know he knows my love because when I put him in his bed he turned completely around in a circle to face me, but when I put him in bed with me he didn't move at all because he felt secure because he knew my love was close. He knows the feel of my love and I know he knows it is not there and I can only imagine how he is acting because of it. This little boy is good for a protest. He finally decided to let me change his diaper without straightening his legs so I couldn't do anything. But he would still cry in protest almost every time. He was even so strong by now that he would jump off the diaper because he didn't want to deal with that whole process. And as he got nicer he stopped peeing on me. I miss and love my little Mo Mo. He is so special.

April 23, 2007—Monday—1:12am

I am feeling kind of stunned. I went to church today and was obedient to God and talked to Pastor William about starting a school. I had a dream the other night about working in an office and it was not good. But soon after that I had a dream about getting a teaching job and I made a lot of money and how weird, but it was in Hollister. Pastor William referred me to Wilma

Simpson to help with my questions. I am thinking of attending her brother's service on Wednesday and later asking her questions about starting a school. I am thinking of changing the service I attend to the 9am service on Sunday. Of course I am trying to get away from someone. I realize it wasn't everyone I was hiding the baby from but only people I didn't care much for. I felt like the bad energy from the bad people would get on him. I believe he is coming back, but I still miss him. I realize I have to be careful of what I bring into my life. I should look at ways of giving to others but not anything that is going to take up too much space. This is the time I should read my books and listen for messages from God. When I was asked today about the baby I just said that everything was fine and didn't offer anything else.

Tomorrow is the day the Virginia Tech students return to school and it is also the day the baby is four weeks old. Being a mother makes you a better person. I watched a movie tonight and the theme was forgiveness. I can say I've had to focus on forgiveness through this process.

I miss the noise the most. None of the pictures I have of him do him justice. I wish I had one with his eyes open. None capture his true spirit. The closest one is when he is putting up a fuss after we came home from Doctor's Hospital. That had been a long day. We had even been to North Berkeley also. It has only been a week, but it seems like a month.

April 25, 2007—Wednesday—3:23pm

Today is Tabitha's birthday and she is turning two years old and tomorrow Walter will be one month. On Monday when I woke up I asked God what did He want me to know and He told me I needed to clean. I needed to finally wash Mo Mo's last bottle and his dirty clothes and I also needed to clean my house to get ready for the baby that was coming. He told me I needed to be ready before I could receive. At some point I said, thank you God, and did a little dance because I knew in my heart it was true. To confirm what I felt, I read my daily devotional from Joyce's book. It also said to clean the vessel.

Tuesday was the first day I did not look at Mo Mo's pictures and there were no clothes to smell. His little energy was gone. But I know in my heart someone is really on the way. On Monday I was frantically cleaning and nervous and kept my cell phone handy because I knew it was going to ring. Tuesday was quiet and peaceful, but I had a dream that concerned me. The idea was there was something in the baby's place so I couldn't receive him. This concerned me so I meditated on it all day searching for the answer. I know this could also represent the presence of something because I believe the presence of my job was so huge it blocked the baby from coming. Because the day after I said I was leaving—a baby became available. This also happened because I was obedient to God.

I wondered if I should put action behind my faith and call the agency and tell them to only send me Walter because there was going to be a call for him. I thought about it and thought about it and on Wednesday morning Joyce had a guest and they were still talking about praying. It came up again that you have not because you ask not, but I was still trying to figure out the rest of my situation. How could I make sure I was available for Walter? So that was my prayer, for God to make sure I am available to receive Walter when the time comes. This way I don't have to miss out on anything or anyone else. As a part of me believing he is coming back, I really felt strengthened because I felt concerned that I told Walter I would be waiting for him. I gave him my word that I would be there for him. I know he heard me because that will be one of the secrets he has and when he can't take it anymore he will make his move to get out. But he needs to know I'm waiting to receive him. Just as it was when I initially received him. I was ready for him. Even though I have been really quiet I can feel a baby coming, maybe even before the week is out. There is a part of me that just wants to call the agency and tell them I'm waiting for Walter only, but does that mean I am not trusting God?

April 26, 2007—Thursday—10:10pm

I am having an anxiety attack. My heart is beating fast and I am breathing rapidly. Today Walter is one month old. I have not looked at his pictures since Monday. I woke up today and I felt like God was telling me to start a school in my apartment. A combination of that and what I can do to help my student, Tiffany, and if the baby is coming back is freaking me out. I am led to believe he is coming back because all I have heard is I have to ask, but Wow. Generally, God tells me exactly. Another thing that is freaking me out is the book God had me to read about a woman who has the same birthday as me and there was a boy named Walter who came to her. But he did not stay. I am asking God point blank right now if he is coming back. If I had read the book ahead of time, I would have really been freaked out because he would have come and matched the name in the book. The hard part about this whole thing is that it's between me and God. God please guide me. Please give me peace and please give me the strength to follow Your will.

April 30, 2007—Monday—3:13am

I miss my mother because I could tell her everything. I was the center of her world and she always had time for me. I could really use that right now because I feel I am about to turn another corner in my life. I am about to move to another level with God and loving. I am actually going to let someone into my sanctuary—my secret place. I believe God has been telling me to do this, but I was not emotionally ready for it. But now that Walter has kicked down some of the walls to my heart, I am now more willing to give and love. Maybe that's one of the reasons God brought him into my life. Because after I turned in the last work for my job is when he left as to say, it's now time to focus on something else. He really helped me to change my value system. Love needs to be a part of it. The thing I am longing for in my life is to love because that's where the true love in life comes from. Walter did that for me. He also helped my ability to love by learning better to forgive. He literally left his foot prints in my life. He was the perfect and special baby to do that. He was from God. I can never forget him for that, but I do need to have room in my heart to continue to love others and to receive love. I now open my heart to any baby who needs my love and I will let God work out the details.

God is asking me to check myself and understand if I am letting these kids in for the right reason. I have searched my heart and know I want to help these children. I want to give them a safe place to grow up, to talk about things that are important to them and to learn about things they might not learn elsewhere. These are things that will help them to move through life with confidence and understanding. I wonder who would want to come. I am hoping they will want to come.

I believe this is where God wants me to start in order to develop the character I will need later. My success in this would help to determine my future. I believe He wants me to take this step and the rest will work itself out. I wish I had someone to share this with. Maybe after I have taken the steps to get it going I will then share with people what I am doing. I just want everything to go well. When you tell people things you have to listen to their opinions. I don't want to hear that right now because I need support right now and anything else would be a distraction. I know what I went through with the baby thing and that was lesson enough.

I stood in my living room yesterday and realized even though everything was neat and clean I wanted something else in my house and that was love. I realize having the kids in my home would not just be about what I wanted to do, but also what they wanted to do.

I must go to church every Sunday because that is the anchor in my world. God is telling me to not commit to anything with Tiffany, but for this week to give her $20 for food and see how that goes. I can't commit to having her over for dinner because that might interfere with the baby that is on the way.

May 5, 2007—Saturday—2:49am

My response to today is totally unexpected. It got a little loud so I thought I would have had more of a response of relief after the kids left, but it was just the opposite. After I said thank you and good-bye to the kids and parents downstairs and I came in here to my quiet little apartment—it took me a minute to figure out what was going on with me. But it didn't take too long because the feeling was familiar. I was alone and lonely and depressed. What kind of response is that? Everything again was clean and quiet, but missing the love.

I am looking forward to the day when God sends me the baby that is supposed to be in my care because this new feeling is now pleasant. It will also be beautiful to have all of the kids here together. God I believe is tampering with my heart. He is teasing me with love. I know the kids had love in their hearts today because they didn't even want to leave. They all stood around and delayed. That made me feel great. I had accomplished something great today. I am so thankful to God for leading me to this place of love. It is only because I know now what love is that I can miss it. This is unbelievable to me that this is happening to me. I never thought I could want someone in my life so badly.

The kids were thankful because Josie even said she would keep her mother's candle in her bedroom as if she thought it was something special. When she came in the door she said my house smelled like her grandmother's house. She also said my place was nice like a college dorm. I know it was a compliment. I believe she meant it was cozy.

Bunny asked if I had kids, so I told them about what happened with the baby. That was the reason why the bottles were made is because the day the baby left, I was expecting him to come home with me. She asked me if I was sad and I said yes. She asked how old the baby was when I got him and how long did I have him. She also said she didn't understand how someone could carry a baby for nine months, go through all of that pain and then walk away from it.

Joshua was the perfect gentleman by pouring the beverages for the young ladies and letting me walk out of the door before him when we were leaving. His mother did say he had been bugging her to remind her that he was coming.

All of the kids were very nice and enjoyed themselves and that was a special feeling for me. We started off everything with a prayer and blessing the food. I thanked God for bringing them all to my home and that we would all get what we were supposed to get from it. Joshua asked me why I just don't come and hang around the school. The kids even admitted he looks like my brother and he was not offended. Josie let me count their money from the game of Life and that was a sweet gesture. They were open to accepting help. This is one of the most fabulous things I have done in my life and I thank God for it. Something I noticed when the kids were leaving is that when I closed with a prayer they continued to sit as if they wanted to pray longer. I simply thanked God for bringing us together and for Him to guide all of us in the coming days and we should continue to honor Him. Eventually, I would like each of them to lead the prayers.

I know I was truly depressed afterward because I retreated to my safe place—my bedroom and I have felt it all through my body, an indescribable tiredness.

It was also very kind of them not to rush me when they were waiting to play the game of Life. Bunny gave me the card of the teacher and said it must be my destiny to be a teacher. I think it was Bunny that said I shouldn't feel bad that I don't have cable TV because she doesn't either.

May 10, 2007—Thursday—2:20am

I don't believe this is happening to me. Pastor John last night spoke to me about his concerns about my relationship with students. This has to be one of the craziest things I have ever heard. I can understand a part of what he was saying, but the truth is he does not want me there and I can understand why. I don't work for him when I'm there at the church. I work for God. I am there to serve God not him. I am led to take my own advice and handle problems immediately. This leads me to talk to Pastor William to ask his take on the situation. I knew my day of conflict was coming and I am flattered because this validates for me I am doing a great job for God. This incident is to only serve as a distraction. My options are to speak with Pastor William or wait on God and possibly not return to the

Wednesday night meetings. I fear the results because this would be a test of Pastor William's character and I know he is only a man.

I thank God for bringing me where I am today and I look forward to my continued journey with Him.

May 13, 2007—Sunday—4:17am

I hate Mother's Day and here it comes again. Every year I deal with celebrating it in a way that acknowledges women that in no way love me as much as my mother did. My mother was the best woman I have ever known. She was strong, smart, beautiful and talented. I don't know a woman who can compare to her. This is a feeling I don't even think my brothers can understand because they didn't love my mother the way I do. I hate Mother's Day because no other woman can compare to my mother.

This week was emotionally very challenging for me because of the incident at church and working as a substitute teacher. These were things to shake my core. I am wondering how I can manage working as a substitute teacher. I know God will work it out. I also realize my situation with the church has to do with me being able to forgive. Pastor William says you can forgive, but you don't have to continue the relationship in the way that it was. I am going to trust God to lead me to the proper way to continue. I guess I am truly a follower of Christ to address this situation because generally I would just walk away.

I wish God would tell me what He wants me to do so I can feel fulfilled. None of the other kids showed up on Friday, so from now on I am just going to let it be me and Bunny. I am not going to push for anything. This does create a bit of pressure to do things with Bunny that are meaningful. As long as I stay connected to God I will be okay. I'm also wondering what God is going to do about me having a baby. He has now given me the desire. I know that means it will come. It makes me think of what my brother says about God works in order. Is He waiting for me to get a husband or to get steady work? I hate Mother's

Day.

May 14, 2007—Monday—4:25am

Yesterday I got the idea to go to South Africa to help the youth. Missionaries came to the church and it just felt right. The thing that struck me as unusual is they asked if there was anyone who wanted to go back with them, should speak with Pastor William. I was at the morning service because of my weird sleeping habits and also so I could drop off my Mother's Day stuff and get back home. While I was driving to Courtland I realized this was something I wanted to look into. I ran my errands, went home and changed clothes and caught one of the missionaries after the second service. I asked Pastor William if they had already gone because I was interested in speaking with them. I told him this seemed like a good idea because this would be meaningful work. He actually agreed.

After speaking with the woman I didn't feel too informed, but before we parted she looked into my eyes and smiled and said some things I can't remember and gave me a long embrace. It was as if she knew she would see me again.

I know where I am today is because of little Walter. Today I cried because I know it's true. He gave my life purpose and since he's gone I have been searching for that feeling again. There has not been anything else in my life that has felt so meaningful and fulfilling and I believe the experience in South Africa would give me that sense of purpose again. Just like with Walter, it was challenging, but in the end it broke my heart to not be able to give that much love to anyone. Through loving him I never thought I would be willing to touch poop or look in someone's toosh. But I did it all for Walter and that was true love. I am not looking to receive love. I'm looking to give it.

Today I met a young man in the store who was carrying a large pack of beer. He wanted to talk to me and gave me his telephone number. I immediately knew I should not talk to him, but after I took a nap and woke up I realized God had said to increase your circle of love. On Sunday it was Joel's message as well as

Joyce's. What a coincidence. I guess I'm supposed to talk to this young man.

My thoughts about Africa are that if everything falls into place for September then it is meant for me to go. Because I don't have any commitments for the fall.

May 15, 2007—Tuesday—10:50pm

I am currently hoping for a trip to South Africa. Before I went to sleep last night I listened to Joyce and she said to not miss out on opportunities. And sometimes you have to act quickly because you might miss the opportunity and it might not come again. I apply this directly to—do everything in my power to go to South Africa. It is also funny that yesterday when I was renting my tapes from the library a woman was presenting that night on Africa. The message I got from Joyce is the same message I got from my mother after she passed—to take advantage of the opportunities that present themselves. Because I am likely to go—God has told me to focus on money. So I have booked sub work for the rest of the week and Monday and Friday of next week. God is truly being good to me.

I got great news today that my back teeth are strong enough to hold a stay plate, so it looks like I will be able to smile on my birthday. Wow, I will now appreciate smiling again. This also means I will be able to pay off my new teeth. Praise the Lord for progress. I also believe I will be able to speak properly and stop drawing such weird attention to myself and truly be prepared for summer school. You have to love a Lord like this one.

May 17, 2007—Thursday—12:09am

I had yet another fabulous day. I say fabulous day because when I called to check on my apartment lease the expiring date is 8/31/07. This is the perfect date because I could then leave at the beginning of September. This is one of the signs that everything is lining up. The storage compartment I need is affordable also. I sent off my e-mail to the missionaries with hopes to hear from them soon. Alexis even asked if there was anything she could do to help. It also seems everywhere I turn I keep hearing the message to take advantage of opportunities all around me, even on TV commercials.

Just like Joyce said, be careful what you think because the devil is trying to make me think things are too good to be true. Today while subbing I have seen students I knew a few years ago and this makes me feel subbing has turned into a good way to leave the district or at least leave the country.

I am also following what Joyce said about doing what's right even if you feel wrong. I went out of my way to speak to Pastor John tonight even when I didn't want to. He seemed a little not himself tonight, not really up. I could be wrong, but I'm thinking it's because of the situation from last week. He didn't say anything to me about it, but he knows what Pastor William said to me so I guess it's just understood that I have done nothing wrong. I also attribute to Africa the opportunity for obedience to God because after I stood up for myself and talked to Pastor William, the next opportunity presented itself. I am proud of myself for how well I am handling this. It is obvious I have grown.

May 17, 2007—Thursday—10:41pm

Even though the group that came to the church is not going back to South Africa for two years, God is still telling me there is an opportunity coming my way. Today I followed that idea and paid for my passport and all of that fell into place. The kids at Howard were great and I got there late, but the teacher didn't have a first period class.

I am thinking of contacting Joyce for my missionary assignment. God is also telling me it is okay that Friday is working out the way it is. The devil is trying to make me think something is wrong.

My epiphany for today is—there have been people in my life that really care about me. It's just that people do the best they can. Their character flaws were the things that made things seem otherwise. Forgiveness is important. God please help me to think better of other people and to be a better person myself.

May 21, 2007—Monday—12:49am

I have just finished working on my hair again after chopping it off. I kind of did a Britney Spears. This is how I can relate to what she did. After certain life changing events and circumstances, you change inside which causes you to have a strong desire to make a change on the outside. I was tired of the grease and weight of my hair. Even though it was a short do, the time it took to put the grease in my hair in the morning was getting to be too much for me. The maintenance of it was time consuming also. I was very distracted by the ends that were standing up straight and not curling. During this time of the season my hair was growing really fast and feeling extra thick. This causes it to feel dirty more often.

Before I cut it, I was having visions of short hair to my head. Especially when I thought of myself in Africa. I saw myself with a bald head and a big smile. As a part of me cutting my hair and getting adjusted, I had to put some touches on it to make it more presentable for the public. This is very important because I will be around those kids tomorrow and I need to feel as well put together as possible.

The funny thing about this process is I was trying to make my hair do something it didn't want to do. I was brushing it back. That's the direction it was going before I cut it off. When I was doing that, it just didn't work. My hair didn't look as good as I knew it could. But once I decided to comb it in the direction it wanted to go in, I ended up with a really cute hair style. The waves fell into place all over my head. I put a line as a bang and my baby hair for side burns and the front area remained intact and in place. It is amazing what can happen if you do what you are supposed to do.

I am now trying to figure out what God wants me to do with my life. Joyce in her Friday message said to have a plan and that was the same message this Sunday in church. I need to be sure of what God is calling me to do then get to it. I realize it may require some faith, but if it is what God asks me to do I know it will be great in the end.

The idea of Africa was presented, but it fell through and now I don't know what God wants me to do. But I do know an opportunity is coming and I need to be prepared to take it.

May 22, 2007—Tuesday—12:19am

Monday was a hoot. There was a mix-up at Penbrook so I was able to have the day off after all. I took a drive to Oakland to take my purse back to the repair shop because God has not approved me to buy anything new. I went to Lee's and he gave me the name of some people who could repair my muffler for a lot cheaper than him. I got my car repaired for so little money it's not funny. Even though I'm bald, I guess I'm still cute. I had a fabulous day running around being productive. I took some of Mo Mo's formula to a new mother in a shelter and she really appreciated it. I will be glad to find out what I am supposed to be doing with my life. Right now I believe God is giving me the okay to stop attending the Wednesday night service at church because my time is done there.

Today when I stopped at the school to pay for my yearbook, I saw Harrison. I know he saw me too. I think he was trying to wait to talk to me, but he had to help a student. Our connection is still there because I could feel him. I still wonder if he is the one. I am currently afraid of my feelings about men because I am feeling tempted. This makes me not want to talk to anyone because of my hormonal issues. I have to really stay in the Word to keep me grounded at this time. God please help me.

May 23, 2007—Wednesday—12:18am

What a day. My day was very long at Porter, but most of the kids were good. I followed that up with a visit to Dr. Wilmington and he was not too pleased with me. I cried in his office. I am noticing most times I am thinking when something is wrong it is my fault or something I did. An example of this is the situation with Bunny's mother. Even though I know I did nothing wrong, intentionally, I questioned myself. When Alejandra and Alexis said they both didn't have my number because of a new phone—I felt like they just didn't want to talk to me. I really must deal with my self-esteem and confidence.

I have recently had incidents where I felt a little scatter brained. This substantiates that I need down time in order to collect myself. I am desperately feeling that now because I am feeling so confused about my life. I am so unsure about what God wants me to do in my life.

On Monday I gave some formula to a woman in a shelter and the next day I got a call about a baby. I think God is trying to tell me one is still coming, but I don't understand any of that. Am I supposed to become a missionary or am I supposed to teach full-time in the fall? Today Mo Mo's picture fell and I put it back up and by the time I got home from work it had fallen again. What the heck does that mean? I left it laying there in a twisted way. I feel so confused that I can't offer anyone advice on anything. I am trying to decide what to do about tomorrow. Do I go to the church and say goodbye and clear up issues with kids or do I just not go? I think it's the right thing to do—to clear up things and then not go anymore.

May 24, 2007—Thursday—12:12am

Today was another spectacular day in the life of Shella Bridgeman. I had two opportunities to speak to students regarding what it means to be a Christian. Wow, how powerful is that! Now that I think about it, this is what this whole Christian thing is about. I liked having that conversation with the kids about how this whole thing goes. Maybe there's something to this subbing? A whole lot more than I thought. What happened today answered the question for me about the Wednesday night deal bearing fruit. I now know for sure that it is. Hallelujah, I guess I finally have one thing figured out.

God has also told me not to give up on the baby thing, but to keep all of the baby stuff I have. Probably one of the most important things I need to do right now is to focus on God and His love for me. This will increase my confidence, which will make me comfortable in life. Today I'm glad I ran into Ms. Draper regarding my current situation. I feel like I have now gotten rid of my dirty little secret. I'm looking forward to the holiday weekend to be able to spend that time with God. My next goals are to read the entire Bible and Joyce's Battlefield of the Mind. I know this is where God is leading me.

May 27, 2007—Sunday—12:22am

It looks like I'm going to Africa, South Africa specifically. I was led to call my friend who used to be called Harriet who is now Anastasia. Somehow I slipped and mentioned Africa and she suggested that I contact Oprah to join her school. I have to admit I had thought of contacting Oprah and even my kids suggested I go and work with Oprah in South Africa. Anastasia mentioned something about Alice in Wonderland and how once you've started going down the rabbit hole there's no turning back. This means once you've become aware on a certain level you can't go back to where you were. I talked to her about Africa because she mentioned she would be leaving on September 1st and I told her that was the day I had planned on going to Africa.

Against my better judgment, I later called Troy to check in with him. We talked a bit and I told him I thought I was going to be leaving the country and he said, "Where, Africa?" I thought that was the weirdest thing he could have said of all places, Africa. After we continued to talk he mentioned he knew two people that had gone to Africa and both said they felt fulfilled. This was the key word he said to me because this is exactly what I'm looking for. Since Walter, I have no choice but to live a life of purpose.

Later on I was watching Star Trek of all things and keep in mind it was the original Star Trek with Captain Kirk on channel forty-four. There was another mention of Alice in Wonderland. This was a definite sign God was guiding me.

I believe God is leading me to South Africa, but I still keep getting the message to have a plan.

Just as I was writing this I remembered Troy said his friend was working on building a hospital. Who knows, maybe he and I can do some work together. Maybe it's our destiny.

Also how did I see the tail end of the Will and Grace Show and they were using silly string and then later I saw a commercial and people were using silly string? God is telling me I am exactly where I am supposed to be and He is leading my steps.

May 28, 2007—Monday—1:14am

I received another message today about Africa. I turned to channel nine because somehow channel seven blacked out while I was watching the Dead Zone. So I turned to channel nine to see the program that evaluates restaurants called, Check Please. There was a reference to Alice in Wonderland.

Last night I heard a minister on TV mention the devil comes in when you're weak. Just like I suggested, Troy called today, but he knew it was wrong so he didn't even leave a message. He called at four something. I was pretty sure he would call too. I was already prepared to not talk to him and it was not difficult. I do thank God for leading me to him to continue to be inspired about Africa.

I have eaten an enormous amount of food to help me with these life changing decisions I have to make. I sometimes think of having relationships with people, but when I look at where I am now I know the way I have been doing things is the way it's supposed to be for me. I need to spend the time I do with God. It works for me. The difference maybe between me and my mother is when I reconnect with people after a time I have made changes. Then again, maybe she was making progress also. This reaffirms she was a very spiritual person and her quiet in her life was due to her spending time with God. I believe I will honor my family by serving in South Africa. I will live the intentions of my mother and grandmother. They will be so proud.

I now have a sense of sadness because I don't know when I'll see people again. I am being very mindful of how to proceed and have closure to relationships because I don't know if they will leave this earth before I make it back this way again. I am trying to think of all of the things I want to say to them before it is too late. I feel the importance of this deeply in my spirit.

Tonight I watched a repeat show of Oprah's from earlier in the week about weight loss. I was so amazed at how forgiving she was of a young lady who appeared to not have been doing her best. Oprah didn't kick her out of the program. She gave her another chance. This makes me hopeful that Oprah will give me a chance too.

Yesterday in church Pastor William told a story of one of our church members who extended the offer to a street person to come to church. The homeless man came and gave his life to the Lord. The man then died shortly after that. This touched me greatly because I have been trying to decide if I should contact the young man I met on Mother's Day. By hearing that story it was made clear to me I'm supposed to.

I am getting the message I need to be prepared for the opportunity that is going to present itself to me. Those were the words my mother came back to tell me, but she said to take advantage of opportunities that present themselves. I'm sitting here watching Byron Allen and LL Cool J just came on and spoke to the message I keep hearing about. He said to make sure you have a plan. Because if someone asks you to go to the gas station and you say yes, then you just end up at the gas station. But if that's not a part of your plan then you just say no. He also mentioned that if people don't support your dreams to get rid of them. This for me relates to my brothers. I believe they are toxic. I think it's good we are on speaking terms, but I believe we are back to where we were before my mother's death. They don't fit into my plans.

May 28, 2007—Monday—6:55pm

I had a really depressing day. I need to hurry and find me a job that is relevant and makes good use of my abilities because I don't know how much longer I can put on this charade. I am in desperate need of a meaningful life. Today I saw a Hispanic man in the store holding the most beautiful baby boy that looked to be not more than a month old. I told him congratulations and I really meant it. I was actually glad for him and not jealous. It felt good.

Today Mo Mo's picture fell again and I don't know what it means.

May 31, 2007—Thursday—12:36am

Last night I went to the meeting at the church for the youth. It was interesting as usual. I am only going to serve God and I try my best to do it in a good way. I think I'm hanging in there pretty good in spite of everything that has happened. One student no longer speaks to me. I had a run in with the pastor that is over the youth and I am quite busy with other projects in my life.

Tonight I came home and called Alejandra because I didn't want her to feel I was rejecting her. I explained to her all of the things I am currently working on with the intention of letting her know I am busy. I hope she doesn't just flat out think I am avoiding her. I went out of my way to do that because I know how it feels to be rejected. She is a very nice person, but a part of me still thinks she is gay and that makes me feel a bit uncomfortable. I really felt that way tonight when she mentioned she had called me last night and asked where I was. That statement felt a bit gay as lesbians tend to be a bit possessive. I also noticed last week how when I was talking to the kids she was walking behind me very closely as to hear what I was saying to them. I am going to give her some space, but I have covered it up with the critical life things I need to deal with. I still think she's a nice person, but I think she's a bit sneaky and that gay thing means she is dishonest about who she really is. There is nothing really feminine about her. She really appears mannish. She even walks like a dude, as Creed would say.

My Testimony

Yesterday God gave me the day off and when I woke up at 10:10am and turned on Joyce she was giving the talk about missed opportunities. This was a clear message to me from God that I needed to get on the stick about this Africa trip.

I think I might need to apply for medical to get my teeth, get my shots for the trip and a supply of medicine to take with me.

May 31, 2007—Thursday—11:57pm

Tonight I had an attack of pain in my shoulder. This was caused by stress. I'm trying to find out information for my trip, find a summer job, work for the rest of the school year and figure out what I'm going to do tomorrow. I believe I am supposed to go to the Spring Fling, but I don't want to. I just want to come home and rest.

Today I picked up an application for medical so I can pay for my shots and medicine for my trip. I feel a bit overwhelmed and of course I think it would help if I quit that Wednesday night deal. For all I did today, I feel like I accomplished nothing. God gave me the gift of some good kids today because He knew I needed it. I don't think I've ever subbed and not written at least one referral.

June 1, 2007—Friday—10:36pm

I have recently noticed when things are on my mind, I have to go ahead and write them down so I can think about other things. Today I went to the school for the Spring Fling like God told me to and somehow it was a good thing. I didn't particularly have a good time, but I somehow felt better than I've felt in a long time. I felt rejuvenated. I saw Evelyn and she came running up to me and gave me a hug. That made me feel good because she has always ignored me. That showed me that she really liked me. I saw Dawn and she told me she missed me. Nothing really special happened, but I left feeling really good.

I talked to Ms. James. She came up to me so that means she's not too mad at me for not talking to her anymore or being resistant to showing her the baby. When I told her I was working on going to Africa she was not surprised. She said she had figured that much about what I was going to do. That moment is why I really think I was supposed to go to the school today. She validated for me this is what I'm supposed to do and she also made me think of actually contacting the mission my great aunt founded. I am so grateful to her for her words.

When I walked up to the window in the school's office, the librarian and her daughter were the ones I spoke to. They hit me with the baby questions and I was not prepared for that. But when I think about it that means they didn't know I didn't have him anymore. That means Ms. Downs didn't tell them nor Ms. Draper. That alone made me feel good.

I saw Ms. Jenkins and I was cordial and listened to her quote Scriptures from the Bible and I thought to myself, hum. I didn't go into the school and see any adults, but Ms. Draper would know why and the adults would have to understand I was there to only see the kids. I talked to Ms. Smith and she is really growing with her baby. She is one I hope God is truly looking out for because she really has her hands full. God wanted me to go and somehow I ended up feeling great. Again, I think it had to do with hearing the news about Africa. I am going to follow up with organizations affiliated with my aunt. Through all of that I realized the devil sent some people to make me feel bad about myself and teaching. I just have to know I must follow my passion to teach something other than English. This is something I would like to tell Harrison before I leave is that I want to teach with the passion he has, but something other than English. I want to be a different version of him. I also found myself energized today and wanting to talk to people in a way I haven't in a long time. I even called my cousin three times and he was busy each time. So after I woke up after my nap I decided to catch up on my Joyce program watching.

June 5, 2007—Tuesday—1:37am

Last night I talked to Stephen about my plans to go to Africa. I did this with much hesitation, but it turned out to be the best thing I ever did. Instead of hooking me up with someone who has been before he was able to hook me up with my great aunt's daughter who is still in charge of foundation work for my great aunt's mission. I believe it, but I don't believe this is happening.

Stephen mentioned that I want people's approval, but at the same time I don't. This probably means it would be nice, but I don't care if they don't because I am only living to please God.

While talking to Alejandra tonight, I realized what I had said previously to her regarding my ex-husband was very out of place and cruel. I corrected myself with her because I didn't want her to get the wrong impression of me. I also realize I had spoken out of anger and I did value him as something more than just a crack head. This was a true moment for me to realize I didn't hate him anymore. I guess I have come further than I thought. That was the true test of how you speak of a person. And I even corrected myself. There is a part of me that wants to tell him I forgive him and to almost thank him for helping me to get to where I am today. Everything I have been through has taught me I am strong beyond belief or better yet that God's power and strength can save anyone. If He can bring me through that and fill me with forgiveness and love and strength He deserves to be number one in my life. God saved my life. And I owe Him my life. He saved me and built me up and is preparing me to be an example of what He can do. I am a Bridgeman. I am here to build a bridge for others to God.

I watched Joyce's program tonight and her guest said, because what you most don't want is to be a missionary, is why God wants you to do it. And I said to myself, I know you are not talking to me. God will be clear about what He wants me to do.

I decided to seek the support of my family because I felt God telling me to take the path of least resistance. This means which ever plan works with the least resistance. I didn't feel Oprah was right for me because when I went to her website to send the e-mail there was a limit of 200 characters to be used and it was a small block to write in. The level of importance of this letter for me deserved enough space for it to be formatted properly like a letter and I should be able to make it as long as necessary. I also realized that even though I know Oprah would approve of my message to the kids, she never has mentioned any part of this is a Christian education. This makes me feel that if I got in I would be trying to inspire without saying God. This made me feel like I'd be in the situation I have already been in—to sneak and teach the kids. This became clear to me I am called to teach about God. I will use terms like perseverance, humility, and courage to illustrate the importance of their value and use my life and examples from the Bible to show those traits.

Even though I have all the love in the world for Oprah I can not get behind someone who is living in an unmarried situation and drinks alcohol. But I still love Oprah. But her lifestyle would be a contradiction to what I am led to teach. My thoughts of approval regarding this project are in direct relation to giving glory to God. I want to inspire others to step out in faith to seek passion and happiness.

June 5, 2007—Tuesday—6:04pm

God showed up and showed out again today. I went to payroll today after work to verify receipt of all of my time cards and they were all there. While I was there, I was led to also check on how I would receive my check. The nice new young lady was so gracious to help me and made me aware that I would continue to receive my checks by direct deposit until I told them something different. This was some of the best news I have heard in a long time. This means I have bought myself more time with my bank account situation. And because God is so good to me the bank waived the monthly fee last month even though I hadn't had a direct deposit. When I got home I checked the sub-finder and just like I needed, there is an assignment for Thursday for a half a day. Just like I needed it to be because of my dental appointment on Thursday. This is truly amazing. God I believe is acknowledging my obedience and hooking me up. This is truly awesome. Cousin Candice has not called me yet about Africa. But if I hear what I need to hear from her, I might have to fall out for my life being so great.

My Testimony

June 7, 2007—Thursday—12:59am

Today I talked to cousin Candice about going to Africa. I don't believe this is happening. She said her ex-daughter-in-law is going there at the end of August and I did let her know it coincides with the time my apartment lease expires. When I think about it, it's the time of travel I put on my passport application. I had questions about what I was to do with my stuff and tonight the message at the youth night spoke to selling all of your things and giving the money to the poor and coming to me—which is God. I don't believe this. Pastor John offered to take me to dinner with him and his wife Karen. I could be wrong, but I think it is because there is something they want to talk to me about. I am led to just ask him what it is because I am not really interested in dinner. I will wait and listen to what God has to say, but this is where I'm at with it for right now. I just remembered he asked me about how things were going with my school at home thing and it seemed as though he was really interested. Maybe now that I'm thinking about it he may be actually trying to apologize. Maybe the look on Karen's face last week was in line with an apology. I did notice Zora had the same look of apology. Maybe they want to apologize?

June 7, 2007—Thursday—9:47pm

I don't believe today happened. While I was on break from first period from Hoover for Ms. Parker, I went to the district office to find out the pay for period subbing and to give them my new telephone number. I also needed to find some work for the summer. How is it possible that when I was driving up I ended up driving right in front of Alan Case? Off hand, he said he didn't know who I was, but when I told him he remembered. I didn't know what to expect after that because over the years when I saw him, he never wanted to talk to me. This time he said he had to sign in and then he would come back and talk to me. I waited, but it took him some time so I went and took care of my couple of things and came back. While I was in the office Lori Gutierrez talked to me about her son Raul. Her conversation made me feel she thought I was a fair person. That made me feel good. Connie also saw me and genuinely said she was glad to see me.

After that, I went outside and while I was completing the form he kind of didn't see me and then when he did and started coming towards me, I got a little nervous. I told him when I saw his brother a couple of years ago, I thought it was him or I at least wasn't sure. Come to find out he works in the maintenance department and his brother is a gardener. How weird is that? I told him I have been teaching for about four years and I have been at Crenshaw for three. He seemed genuinely interested. He stared at me intently while I talked to him. He never took his eyes off of me. He was taking it all in. As we talked his phone rang in his pocket and he didn't even look at it. He silenced it and kept talking to me. I think it rang again and he did something to it and resumed talking to me as if it had never happened. He was kind of confused about when I said I was leaving. He was very helpful mentioning options about how I can continue to teach. I corrected him and made him aware that I would be leaving in a few months and maybe I'm being weird, but he seemed sad.

I had to go and he had to go and there was a very awkward moment. He stepped toward me, I think and maybe I stepped back or tensed up. We both started to walk away, but there was something being said with our eyes and hesitation in our bodies that said I want to talk to you again. He must have been nervous about the situation because when he did that thing to his phone, his hand was shaking a bit. He said he would text or call me and I told him texting would not be good for me because I couldn't respond. He said texting was good for him because of nosy people. I asked him if he was really going to call and he gave me a convincing yes. He said it would be either today or tomorrow. Now that I recall more clearly, after I came from the office talking to Lori, his truck was gone.

He looked so good to me. I can see why I was so crazy about him. He was clean and clean cut. His nails were cut down just the way I like them and his goatee was groomed to perfection. It almost looked as fresh as this morning's work. He was casually dressed in a plaid shirt that was tucked in and khaki pants that were not really pressed. But they were obviously clean. As we talked, I got a whiff of a fragrance that almost smelled like Grey Flannel. If I remember correctly that was one of the ones he liked as well as Oscar de la Renta. He wore a pair of moderately stylish glasses. They were a brass color that blended well with his skin color. I complimented him a few times on the glasses and he said they were okay. I also told him he looked good and he said thanks, I think. I really tried not to come on too strong because I had no idea what he was thinking. But when I got that whiff of cologne I wanted to comment and ask him what it was or guess. He kept a safe enough distance emotionally that I thought it best to play it safe. I was just so glad and surprised he was talking to me after all of this time.

I don't think he has a woman because the Alan I knew would have said so and not offered to call me. He said he was just hanging out in Berkeley, like nothing special was going on in his life.

Does this mean I could have called him all of those months ago when the Rocky movie was out and he would have talked to me? I think it happened the way it was supposed to. I am a different person today than I was six months ago. And I think this is the person he will be more pleased with.

Why did God send Alan to me? In what way will he help me? Is he going to Africa with me? Why is my past now in my present? Is God going to be that generous and give me this gift because He appreciates my loyalty so much? Alan never drank or smoke and he was a pretty genuine guy. He was smart, attractive, clean, responsible, honest, interesting, sexual, vulnerable, hard working, and a little hot tempered and loyal. I truly loved Alan and he loved me. The love was real, but that was twenty years ago and maybe I'm being a little hopeful. But maybe we understand things a little better now and maybe we can appreciate each other a little better now. I remember we had a close connection. He understood me and we had a lot of laughs. At forty something maybe we're at the same place in our lives of looking for something more.

He would fit into my plans perfectly because he could come with us to Africa and do the physical part of what we need. He could help with the external aspect of the plan. What is he in my life to teach me? Could this be love again? What I know for sure is he is thinking about this as intently as I am tonight. Alan is a nerd and I now at the age of almost forty-one realize I like nerds. I can remember that he also had class.

I looked for the love letters he wrote to me back when he loved me for sure. I know he remembers everything just like I do. The way we used to eat the Big burgers and call them bricks. The fact that he taught me how to drive a stick shift to the fact that I used to call him Snuggum Booty. I know he remembers just like I do. My tears now are not for pain from the past. It is because of the uncertainty of the future. I loved Alan and I want to know why God is reminding me of this. It makes me long for something I used to have. I remember the day Ms. Draper said to me, his name is Alan. When she said that to me it hit me like a bolt of lightning. I knew she was talking about Alan Case, but I still didn't call him. But God stepped in and brought us together, on this day.

June 10, 2007—Sunday—10:56pm

God has been preparing me for this moment in my life. He has had me to give up everything I valued. First my hair, then my teeth, then my job and now my stuff, including my fancy sports car. The car everybody loves. The one that turns heads. The one that contributes to my million dollar image. It's unique. The design is different from every other car. And it represents me well. This was the one car that showed I had finally arrived—that I was no longer the poor little Black girl from Berkeley.

Letting go of my hair, removed me from the pretty girl status. As an African-American woman, one of your traits of beauty is the length of your hair and I had it.

Another thing that made me who I am is my teeth. The beauty of my smile was in my teeth. This was another part of my appearance that set me above other people.

And the last is my stuff. I have the cool furniture that matches and shines and represents class. It's not the most expensive, but it's nice enough that it represents me well.

Because I love God and am willing to do anything He asks, I will and have given up those things. My job as a teacher was another of those sacrifices made for God. Being a teacher is a status symbol. They don't make much money, but it is a well respected job and people think you're smart. On this job I also had medical insurance and power—even though I did my best to represent God well as a Christian. As a matter of fact, things I taught my former students are things I can use in a Christian setting. But God took me from a full-time teacher to a lowly sub. But I am grateful that it all worked out.

And now here I stand on the eve of being reunited with my love... He was the best man I ever had. As Joyce says, God speaks to you in your gut and I believe there is a huge reason for Alan and I to be reunited. We are evenly yoked as some would say, equally attractive, intelligent, and successful. And I believe a part of this attraction is we are at the same place in our lives. In my heart I will know what to do with him. God will reveal it to me. One of the signs will be the flow. It has to flow in order for it to be right. At this point I don't even know what a deal killer would be because I don't know God's true reason for bringing us together. But just like I have been in tuned to all of the other encounters that have recently occurred I will immediately know the purpose for this one. Sometimes the way God works, you think it's one thing and it turns out to be something else. Like with Troy, I didn't know what it was and it was quickly revealed that it was Africa. I know God will lead me and give me the strength to do whatever He wants me to do, even though I know how God works. I have to admit I'm thinking about love with Alan because I refer back to what Ms. Draper said. His name is Alan.

God is pushing me toward Alan, because Saturday morning when I was having a vivid dream about him, I got a text message saying I needed to pay $5 on my phone. This led me to go to the cell phone store that morning. After standing in line instead of using the pay machine or just dropping a check in the box, I found out I had given Alan the wrong telephone number. Finding this out was a gift from God. I intensely said, he does love me but just didn't have my phone number to call. I associate the correction of the number with him because the clue of correction came when I was dreaming about him. Because I have not talked to him immediately this has given him and me more time to think. It has really given me a chance to breathe a bit because of all of the things that are going on in my life. From leaving the country, to working until that time, to seeing Alan and wondering how he fits into this whole thing... My gut tells me he does because why would he talk to me after all of this time. He could have ended it at the conversation on the street. If I know Alan the way I think I do, he must be interested. Because he doesn't waste time. He wouldn't do something unless there is a reason. And he has to remember our past. He must be interested in me, or should I say, us. At this stage in the game with age and also the intensity of our past, he would have to be willing to be serious. With Alan having the spirit of an adventurer, I'm sure it peaked his interest to hear me say I was leaving all of this behind and going to Africa.

I am so freaked out about all that is going on in my life right now. It's all good and I know God can create these miracles, but it's all happening at once and I'm trying to keep up. I have seen the affects of my love for Alan in my appearance. My love hormones have been released and my face has a glow.

It just occurred to me after watching the Dead Zone that what if this thing with Alan and me is about me doing something for him instead of him doing something for me? I am so stressed that my chest is hurting. I'm going to try listening to one of Joyce's tapes to calm me down.

June 11, 2007—Monday—11:26am

Today I called Alan to give him my correct telephone number. I am subbing at Del Mar and there are no students here, so I did this while I was sitting in an empty classroom by myself. I have the district listing of telephone numbers, so I called. I dialed the number and put in the extension. I was expecting to speak to some receptionist person or something, but he answered. Looking at how he works, I'm surprised he was there. He put me on hold and was having a cool conversation with co-workers, which means he has a pretty decent relationship with them. He was always that kind of person.

I told him I was calling to give him the correct number and he made a sound that indicated he knew because he had tried to call. I asked him if he remembered me telling him I had just changed my number and that was how I made the mistake. He said he didn't remember. But he also made a sound that let me know he understood. He put me on hold again then came back and I gave him the number. I told him the last two numbers had been transposed as he could see when he corrected the number. I wanted to ask him when he would call and I think he could feel I wanted to ask, so he said he would talk to me later which I clearly understood as later today. I said okay and he said bye in a very upbeat way which let me know he was in a good mood in response to my call. I could feel the connection through the phone line that he wanted to talk to me as much as I wanted to talk to him. He has had a chance to think about things just like I have and it has all come back to him as well. And he has put it all in perspective just like I have. We had something great twenty years ago. I'm sure we can only imagine what we can have now as full grown adults. We have both had a journey and I can only imagine what he has seen and experienced since me.

I have lost two babies, had a failed marriage, lost two parents, stopped and started talking to both brothers, graduated from college, twice, moved back to my hometown, gotten saved, joined a church, become a foster parent and am now preparing to leave the country to serve the Lord full-time preaching the gospel. What a journey. Let's not forget—cut all of my hair and nails off and lost a few teeth. What changes have been made! I can say after all of this, I am a different person in some respects. A more accurate statement might be, I'm a better person.

Lord is this really happening? Have you sent my love to me to have? I can't think of anything at this point that would make this a deal killer for me. I have had hope that a man would come, but who knew it would be one I have already loved.

June 12, 2007—Tuesday—1:51am

Alan did not call me like he said he would. I would like to give him the benefit of the doubt. Or is it as they say on the Oprah Show that he's just not that in to me? I have not gotten a clear sign this is not for me to do, but I think I will know more once we talk. But just like Eloise said, he didn't have to take my number he could have just said good bye—it was good seeing you. She said he could be thinking of rekindling our love. I believe I am right on track with what I'm thinking as I have been with the rest of my relationships—even the invisible ones, like Harrison. I was always sure of what was going on even though it was hard for others to understand. I always knew what was going on with me and my loves. This includes Bishop and Ron. In all of these relationships there was always a time later when the truth came out and it was stated that other people couldn't understand.

Alan probably thought he had gotten off the hook when he couldn't reach me last week. He was probably relieved. He could have not called tonight because he just wasn't ready. He probably had to recover from last week and get the courage up again to call. For all of these years, he knows I have never stopped caring about him and he is asking himself if he is ready to jump into this again. The other part of the scenario is I am leaving. A part of that bothers him, but the other part of him wants to go because he is an adventurer. He wants to go with me. But I'm sure he wants to know if I love him that much. So I feel I'm going to have to put my cards on the table as soon as possible to give him time to chew on the <u>truth</u>. The truth is I still love him and I would marry him, but we would have to do it in Africa so's not to mess up our paperwork. The other thing is God is the most important thing in my life.

At this moment, I am led to think of Tony and how he married that woman just after we broke up. Men are looking to feel something in particular and if a woman comes along at the right time and makes him feel that special way, she can have him. Is this that special time in Alan's life? Is his heart vulnerable? As he told me, he is just hanging out in Berkeley. It would be beautiful for us to start a new life together in Africa. I know I was not desperate for a man because I would have bitten on supermarket guy or even considered it. Alan is special. He was, twenty years ago, and I know he still is. And I'm sure just like me he has only gotten better.

I am overwhelmed at the idea of having a quality man in my life—a potential life partner. I already know what he is about. I could possibly have someone to take this journey with me, to share the second part of my life with. Alan is a keeper, but I have to admit the one concern I have is his temper. I want to be in his arms and feel his love. I want to have that moment of truth between us when we share our feelings about being reunited and about what a dream come true it is and truly a fairy tale ending. Alan is an opportunity as well. He will not pass this way again. He is probably more frightened than I am about this whole thing because I was the one who cheated on him. And he has to wonder, is she still like that? But I believe he thinks something different because he has seen the big gold cross on my neck and I told him I was going to probably sell my stuff in search of a more meaningful life. All of that says a lot. That maybe I'm a quality person and a loving person and a risk taker but also serious. These are qualities I'm sure he will find appealing. But in the back of his mind, he's saying, but she's leaving. I think he feels if I'm as good as he thinks I am then he will see this as an opportunity for him as well. Though there was drama in our past he knows there was still a special love.

As I think of him now, I can visualize me living the details of a romance novel and lying back in his arms and exhaling and knowing that was a moment my spirit had been patiently waiting to have.

I ask myself if God is that good. I know that He is, but did He bring me this gift at this perfect time for this special purpose?

Alejandra was just mentioning God's Timing. I feel in my heart this is as important to me as it is to him and I am going to trust my heart on this. I'm sure someone has loved him and broken his heart within twenty years time, but if he is willing to talk to me now that says a lot. Because I was kind of part of something bad. So if he's been through all of these things and now sees me as something good then I know it is genuine because he has had lots to compare me to. I'm sure he is aware of the same thing about me. That I've had lots to compare him to and after all of this time I still like him. It must be real. I know the compliments I gave him have made him aware that I'm interested in him, for sure, even though I'm leaving. The fact that I called Monday morning to give him the correct number shows him I'm interested. He knows for sure how I feel. But he may not know I would marry him tomorrow and I want him to go to Africa with me. But again, I know emotionally he is exactly where I'm at. That's why we met each other again. This was created by God. And I don't know how spiritual he is, but he has to know too that this is from God.

I feel sorry for him for the position he is in. The ball is truly in his court. He knows how I feel. But him actually calling me admits his feelings for me. And again, at this stage in the game, meaning us being in our forties and having experienced all of this life, this is a big deal. I am trying to patiently wait for my love to call, but I think it's important for me to tell the truth. He is probably feeling the same thing and he won't have to be the person to put it out there first. This will validate that I am sincere. This is an opportunity. Therefore, I need to act fast. God will show me the way as He will him. Because this is His work. There were too many things at work for us to show up at the same place at the same time and for the physical encounter to be one that I literally crossed his path. This is God at work.

June 12, 2007—Tuesday—9:16pm

I am so sad because he has not called me yet. I was so sure he felt the way I did. I created this whole thing in my mind about how he had come into my life to go to Africa with me. Based on the negative stories I've heard about this adventure, I thought it would be nice to have company and to make it a little better. Has he not called because he's just not into me or could it be some strange phenomenon that he lost his phone and the paper that has my number on it?

Today I was sure he would call and I said to myself if he didn't it was okay because he just wasn't as smart as I thought he was by passing me up. But now after I go to sleep and wake up and he still hasn't called, I feel hurt. I thought this was to be—that we would have one happy ending. Was this God or the devil? If it is God there is a reason and a lesson. But if it's the devil than it is clearly only a distraction. I hope God will reveal this to me quickly because I am truly sad and it is consuming my thoughts. Maybe I just answered my own question—it was only a distraction. If that is the case someone is playing dirty because I really do love him. I can truly say that because true love never dies. Even though I don't know what he's been doing for the past twenty years, I still love him. This hurts for someone to dangle this man in front of me. But I have to think too about distractions because there was the store guy, then Grant who appeared from who knows where then Mr. Alan. Someone pulled out the big guns on me because he has really gotten my attention. I don't know what I will do next and only God has the answer to why this has come to me. I had thought of him before Africa was even an idea. That makes me think this was God. There were so many things that were leading me to him, but I didn't have the courage to call. So is this a mishap that he hasn't called? But it really is God.

The advice I would give to a friend in this situation would be to wait and see. Based on the prior history and sign from God, I would give it a chance, but don't lose focus of the other things you're working on in your life. But after all of that, I come back to actions speak louder than words. But if he had said the same thing about me then where would we be? The wrong phone number thing with me was a mishap. Even when I go back to him not being mad that I called him at work—something is wrong with this pattern. Why has he not called?

June 14, 2007—Thursday—1:46am

I thank God for this day. I made it. I made it to the youth service at the tail end, but I still made it. There Pastor John and I discussed a few things and I humbly declined his offer to have dinner with him and his wife. He said his reason for asking me was to get to know me better so he could appoint me as a disciple. He clearly said it was not for the purpose of an apology. In my mind while I heard those words, I said wow. He really doesn't have a clue. But I thank God for giving me the strength to continue His work in spite of an uncomfortable situation.

I have had to make the statement to people...I work for God not anyone else, not a church and not a person. God gives me my assignments directly and I don't need anyone's approval to carry them out. I am glad I am not offended by another person's inability or lack of knowledge. He admitted that he knows I've done good work with some of the young people, but he feels he needs to get to know me in order to approve of me. Prior to our misunderstanding, I was giving him information about myself. But at this time, I don't think it's a good idea to open myself up to him anymore.

I thank God for not talking to Alejandra about my conversation with Pastor John. I didn't complain to her or expose the fact that he still had not seen it fit to apologize to me and he feels the need to approve of me. I also got the impression she didn't believe the phone company had given me the wrong phone number—probably because of what I have said about not being bothered.

Today was the last day of school and I feel like a weight has been lifted off of my neck. This led me to finally taking down those baby bottles and getting rid of all of those school schedules. I feel more ready to focus on my other projects like looking for a job here and in Africa. I'm also looking forward to completing my dental work process. I know God is ready to continue blessing me. I even now feel sane enough to bring Alan into my life. I really want to take someone to Africa with me. God really helped me out today.

Today I saw Arturo at the library while I was getting my tapes for West Africa and I asked him to apologize to Donte' and his mother for me. So this has really been a day of letting go. I'm getting a feeling I might be ready to let go of my braces tomorrow.

June 15, 2007—Friday—1:05am

I am so grateful to God for having me exactly where I'm at. I am truly starting over. There is a feel of death to the old life I have known. I am getting rid of all things now and asking for forgiveness of those I have wronged. All of these things are giving me the opportunity to go into my new life with a clean slate. This is how I know it is for me to apologize to Alan and tell him exactly how I feel.

I will apologize to him for not appreciating him fully and hurting him. This I know is of value because pain is something you never forget. I am being given the gift by God to apologize and I know how it feels for someone to admit they have wronged you. Often times we have to just move on in life without the admission of guilt, but it feels better to have the closure with the person.

This is what I feel led to do. I also feel I should confess my feelings to him about how I don't believe it was an accident running into him and he has been on my mind. But I was too afraid of being rejected so I didn't call. I will tell him I know my time is short here, but I would like to spend some time with him getting to know him for who he is today.

With me thinking and feeling all of this right now I know all I have to fear is an opportunity I am not going to let pass me by. Because I know people don't change, I think he might be the one for me, because I get the sense of what we had is still there. After all of what we have been through I think in order for something to happen, I might have to step out of the box and spill my guts. But again, he must be thinking something because he didn't have to offer to call me and I know he did based on his response to the wrong phone number conversation. I remember too at the end of our conversation he sounded happy to talk to me. Who knows why he hasn't called, but I know we can still feel each other. Because he told me he would talk to me later because he knew I was waiting to hear it. He will probably also be glad I left the message for him yesterday because that will let him know for sure that I'm interested. I know he will call today for sure and I can't wait. He probably remembers I'm not patient. So he's probably not surprised I called and left the message. I remember a lot of things about him. I wonder what he remembers about me. I do know he hasn't forgotten, because I can still feel him and he can feel me.

God if you do this for me, I will be very grateful. I also know there has been a timing to all of this because if I had talked to him last week it would not have been the same. Now I have had an epiphany about apologizing and laying my cards on the table. He would also have distracted me from getting through the end of the school year and making my choices about my teeth and tomorrow I will have a job. I had to get some things off of my plate so I could have room for Alan. Now I will. Now I just have to focus on Africa and maybe he will be a part of that journey. God if you do this for me, I will be speechless.

June 15, 2007—Friday—11:57pm

Today I went out and got a job just like I said I would and Alan didn't call. I had a dream today and in that dream mother told me the reason why I hadn't spoken with him was because he had problems he was hiding from me. I can believe this because I know he wants to talk to me and I know he feels me.

Today I got the perfect parking space and walked in that security office and completed a job application. After all of that I was offered a job for the shift I wanted, in the city I wanted and the pay rate I wanted. As I drove home during the traffic hour I felt a huge sense of peace. The highway patrol officer didn't even give me a ticket as I merged from the commuter lane directly in front of him. I waved my hand at him for letting me merge into traffic the way I did. Everything is definitely falling into place.

Later that evening, I watched a program about luck and the woman that starred on Taxi was on the show. She shared how she met her third husband and how over a period of time they were married. The one thing she said that I agreed with is—you have to be prepared, meaning (aware) so when that special meeting comes in your life, you will see it.

I know it was no accident that I ran into Alan that morning. I also know it was no accident that the phone company gave me the wrong number, so I would miss his call. I know it was no accident that when I called to give him the correct number, he answered. And right now that I have still not spoken to him, I know that's no accident either. In my heart, I believe he will call. But it will be at the perfect time. What is God up to with His timing? Some things He is making me be patient for, like my new teeth and Alan. What just hit me is God is giving me everything I need not what I want. I wanted my teeth now, but He's making me wait. But I needed to be approved for the credit for the teeth, so he gave me that now. God does have a sense of humor.

God is doing a work in me because even though my heart aches for love, I am able to be happy for others who have it. Today the San Antonio Spurs won the championship and Eva Longoria's fiancé Tony Parker was on the winning team and voted MVP. They will be married next month on 7/7/07 and I am so happy for them because you can tell when two people are in love. When I see those two together and the way she looks at him, I know they're in love and it makes me know it's possible for everyone. I want Alan and I want a baby. And I don't know what God is going to do about any of this. But I truly feel the purpose for Alan and I seeing each other has not yet been revealed. I have a strong feeling it's not over yet. God didn't do all of this for nothing and to date that's what's happened is nothing. When he calls the first thing I will tell him is I am sorry.

June 17, 2007—Sunday—11:55pm

Today I talked to Carrie about things regarding my brothers and why I can not have a relationship with them. She was very understanding and I don't think she was judgmental about anything I said. My problem is that I spoke ill of people and God has been dealing with me about that. Her response was that I told the truth.

June 26, 2007—Tuesday—3:39am

I have so many thoughts swimming around in my head. Tonight I looked through pictures of my mother and one thing I came up with was she had a weakness for good looking men. When I look at pictures of all of our fathers and other men I know she dated, they all looked the same. They were dark skinned with heavy eyebrows and just handsome. It looks like she continued to date the same guy for most of her life. I guess that's one of the things she passed on to me that I must be careful of.

I have received a clear message about getting rid of things and moving on with my life. I heard the message Sunday in church, from Dr. Wayne Dyer, the show Girlfriends and I have to say, I get it. I feel like I want to hurry up and do it. But it's painful because I'm wondering how much of it I can keep and I'm also having to figure out how to get rid of this stuff. Should I sell it, or give it away and to whom? This is a pretty big assignment, so it's going to take a good amount of patience, perseverance and quiet to figure out how to get this done.

God is dealing with me about my mouth and today it was confirmed because Joyce offered a set of CD's entitled Me and My Big Mouth. I did make it through today without saying anything negative or speaking out of turn. I am feeling a great need to retreat from society because I have serious things I need to work on in order to be ready for Africa. I need to work on my flaws like patience, judgment and faith. I have gotten confirmation again from Dr. Dyer that as a prophet I can not waste my time on trivial life issues. My life is supposed to be about hearing from God so that I may teach others. He made a comment during his program that he is a prophet and he gets paid by the word. I got it. His life's work is about understanding better ways of living and sharing that with others.

He seems to even be consistent with the relationships he has with people so he doesn't give energy to things that are not aligned with his purpose. To do his or this type of work requires support and understanding from the people who are closest to him. Dr. Dyer like myself, is called to a higher purpose and I must give up my things so I can focus on that and not my things.

I am to now be removed from the world. I am not allowed to be in communication with anyone for a good amount of time. I am only allowed when necessary. I am a bit unsure about Wednesday nights, but I think I am to no longer attend because I would have to communicate in order to do it. Eventually I will tell Alejandra about where I'm at with relationships, but I couldn't do that and then see her every week. I did say my goodbyes to the kids last week and I kind of feel my time there has run its course.

I have to admit I keep coming up with trust issues with Alejandra and I don't think that's normal. I feel I should listen to that and leave her alone. I have noticed the habit with Stephen that anything I say he always presents a negative view. This is toxic behavior to sabotage my works. I will soon be in my own world as God has instructed me to do. If possible, I will go to the family picnic and then I will disappear. I need to spend as much time as possible with God and I have to stay away from negative people. Like Dr. Dyer says, I have to have the courage to die while I'm still living. I was so glad to hear this in his program because I know I was feeling death and now I understand why. It is time for me to start over. The apartment complex even gave me the next of kin contact information. I am truly dying to my old self.

I do know it's going to work out, but I realize I must slow my roll so that I will have a place to live. Don't give notice until I have my passport in hand. Come to think of it I need to make sure I have my visa also. I may switch to the month to month lease and pay much more, but I can use the money I will get from selling my stuff to pay the extra for rent—because it looks like I will be able to get my shots for free.

June 27, 2007—Wednesday—4:24am

This morning I put my living room furnishings on sale on Craigslist. I am realizing that I feel nothing about it. This is crazy. I can't imagine for as much as I value my stuff that I feel absolutely nothing. If anything, I'm actually relieved that I finally did it. I can clearly see this assignment is truly from God. At some point I had completed the ad and then lost it. But God helped me to recover it. It was an amazing feat because I have never been able to complete that function on the computer before this incident. I also realize this is from God because the amount of time and patience and concentration it took me to do this, I did need to do it alone. This is a very personal process I need to complete in a special way. It is critical that I have no distractions and stay connected to God. This is the craziest thing I've ever done. But it doesn't feel crazy. It feels right.

Everywhere I turn everything is about Africa. I keep seeing programs on channel nine about Africa—from Africans that have moved to the U.S. to Africans returning to their homes in Sierra Leone. These were very unusual programs because they showed real people and all of the basic struggles they had. The Africans in the U.S. couldn't even open a medicine bottle that was childproof because they had never seen one before. And when they bought frozen Banquet chicken from the supermarket they asked how you could tell that it was chicken. Then they had to figure out how to cook it to eat it.

The people in Sierra Leone lived in a very dismal situation. They moved from the refugee camp to Sierra Leone, their home before the war, and they entered into an unknown situation. They had no jobs and didn't know where they would live, but they had hope. Their music was an important vehicle to keep their spirits up. All things are about Africa on TV every time I look up. God is affirming my destiny to me. I wondered if God was playing one of His tricks on me by having me do all of this for something else. All I know is right now I need to keep going in the direction of West Africa. I also realize I'm not waiting on God. He's waiting on me to be ready to take this journey. There are things I need to work on and the most important thing I can think of is my love walk. This, including my mouth. Yesterday when I was faced with disappointing news from the storage place and sarcasm from Stephen, I held my tongue and didn't complain or say anything negative. So far so good.

June 27, 2007—Wednesday—10:53pm

Today I started clearing out my storage room with the books in it and I had the strangest reaction. I almost started to cry because I was having to give up my prized books. That says a lot about what is important to me. I believe in education and these are things I want my kids to learn. I want them to be well educated and prepared for the world they live in. But what I've noticed is that once you start to purge it's easy to continue. I will be a teacher again someday.

While looking at the books, I admired the wealth of information they contain. This was a very personal process I needed to do by myself to say goodbye to my loves. I put the boxes in my car and started my journey to the Salvation Army and had a great sense of calm about me. I was so calm and relaxed that when it was time to remove the books from the car I barely had enough strength. I was too relaxed. After dropping off the one load I decided to pick up another because I still had time. The second time was easier.

When I came home I continued my dinner for the evening. I also decided I would call Alejandra and say my good-bye. When I spoke with her she said she admired my level of commitment. I laugh now thinking of her telling me that some time ago she held back some of her commitment to God hoping He would not send her to Africa. I laugh to myself thinking, oh no not Africa. Ha. Ha. As I loaded my books on the truck, knowing what I know about how things end up in Africa, I thought maybe I could meet them there or someone there will get them because they need them. My people in Africa need love and help.

When I checked my e-mail this evening I had received two e-mails from people interested in the items I posted on Craigslist. This helps me to believe people will show up and purchase the items. The people that were interested wanted pictures, but I'm sure there are people who read the entire message and will show up because they can tell the items are quality and a great price. I'm looking forward to seeing God show up and show out, on Saturday.

I had an idea today to move into a studio apartment here after my lease expires because it might be a cheaper deal for month to month rent. I would like to pay something a lot more reasonable than $140 more than what I'm currently paying. By that time, if I moved into a studio I would just be moving my bedroom set because I would have gotten rid of everything else. The only thing is I do like the snugness of the location of this apartment. But who knows, maybe again, it's time for me to go. Depending on if I have my passport or not will have a lot to do with it.

June 28, 2007—Thursday—4:51am

Again, everything is coming up Africa. When I turned to Tavis he had a guy on talking about Africa. Then when that went off and I turned to Oprah she had someone on talking about Africa. Then when I flicked back to channel nine the newscaster was talking about Africa. I don't think the message can get any clearer. Somehow I feel led to West Africa and for all of the things that are coming up, I am keeping my eyes and ears open for an opportunity for myself. I have to admit the orphanage I saw on Oprah in Ghana looked great. It would be teaching kids who have been rescued from slavery after being sold by their parents. The kids were so happy and focused and grateful to learn. I know God will show me the way. I just need to make sure I am taking care of what I can on this end. That means getting rid of my stuff and developing my character so when the time comes, I will be ready to go. Praise the Lord.

June 29, 2007—Friday—6:01am

I am led to question the security position I turned down. It was exactly what I had asked for according to location, salary and hours. But I turned it down because I felt uncomfortable. I have to ask myself if any of this was warranted, or was it just fear from my past. To tell you the truth, I feel a little rushed to be leaving by the end of August. That is only two months from now and it feels like a rush to have to get everything in order. I need a job and extra money to take with me and even time to get myself mentally and spiritually ready to go. There are some character traits that need to be in place first and like I said, God doesn't seem to be in any hurry. Is God giving me that age old message, which is to slow down?

I am tempted to call that security site and find out if they have filled that position. For some reason I am thinking the hours were 4pm to 12am. If that is the case it would be a good fit because I could still sub in the fall to make extra money. If I could work the two jobs and make the extra money-that would be fabulous. There is nothing like getting rid of debt. If I had all of that extra money, it makes me think why move to a different apartment. One, because maybe I'm just supposed to move and the other reason is that it would feel kind of weird being in this big apartment with no furniture in it. If I see the guys working over there, I think it would be helpful to see the apartment itself—check out its energy. And if all else fails, I can change my mind.

June 30, 2007—Saturday—5:11am

This is my big day and I have had no sleep. I'm believing this day will go well, but I had a few things to do to get prepared. Everything is ready except the fact that I was unable to collapse the baby bed. I guess it's not time to let it go. Mo Mo wants to keep his presence here a bit longer.

Yesterday I talked to Troy and he mentioned working in Cleveland to me. I have to admit it feels more comfortable than Africa because I know I would be well taken care of, meaning I would have a lot of support. That is the one thing I wanted was to feel like I had someone to trust and help me out. When I think of Africa, I don't get a good feeling about working with my family because no one has ever contacted me about anything. This doesn't make me feel good. I get a bad vibe from the whole thing, but I was willing to go anyway because God was leading me to do so. I had kind of even cancelled them out and was looking for some other organization to go with, but I have been unsuccessful. Yesterday, I was on-line looking for a job in Africa and I noticed a particular organization. Later on I was watching the news and there was that same organization doing work in Cleveland. How freakish is that? I did ask for God to hook me up with a situation that was supportive and stable and then came the idea of teaching in Cleveland. I thought the kids would just be another bunch of ungrateful U.S. kids. But Oprah ran a show highlighting a gentleman who started a program in Harlem which turned kids around. They also showed three African-American teachers who did the same thing with African-American students. I felt that was God's way of showing me it is possible. I finally have a good feeling about something. Now I'm going to go on-line and look for a job. I need it to be Christian based teaching and I would like to teach without having to return to school to further my education. This would fit in with the time my lease expires and I would be ready to start this school year. The timing would be perfect and the plans I have already would not change because I would still only be taking my clothes when I relocate. I am on schedule and ready to do this and I feel secure because I know I will have support. I have to see what God says about this. I think this is what He wants.

July 1, 2007—Sunday—3:11am

Yesterday was some day. I waited a whole day to sell one piece of furniture, but it finally happened. I am probably judging Pastor John when I say that people in teaching positions are held to a higher standard. I pray that he will hear more of what God is saying to him and follow it. He has a critical job with teaching those kids.

Well, I believe God is messing with me. After a super long day, I decided it was time to check the internet to investigate the Cleveland thing. Probably about the second site I went to had a position for a youth pastor in Cleveland. Ha. Ha. The killer part is they had a statement about, not letting fear send you in the opposite direction of where God is calling you to serve. This really was a fact that God was speaking to me because that's exactly what I was talking to Harriet about was—I get what I want, but then my response is fear. Is that what I'm supposed to do? The job posted on May 3rd and it still hasn't been filled. What is that? And does this tie into the fact that I was sentenced to attend the youth night at church? I recently came to the conclusion that a big part of the reason for me being there had to do with learning what not to do. I somehow knew that this was a part of my future to come.

Boy does that have a ring to it, Pastor Bridgeman, or Pastor Shella? I think Bridgeman sounds better. Hey, when I was just talking to Harriet she was just saying that she was getting her papers to be Reverend Harriet and I was asking her questions because it was my desire to become a reverend. What is God up to now?

Did He have me to quit my job, to get the baby, to open me up, to consider Africa, to pursue Cleveland to become a minister? That is a heck of a plan, but it feels good and it feels real. And it makes sense. I see me ministering at this time in my career. I think I'm ready. Only as ready as God has made me is what I mean. It would be something that I would totally lean on Him for. I would still be teaching. I feel like I'm at a place of fully being me—which is all about God. You know it's time when you can't do anything else and that's what I think I mean about being ready. God is my life and that's what I want to live and breathe everyday. I feel at this point in my life it's time for me to share my life with the world in order to continue to grow and have any type of real satisfaction in life. It's time for me to be the real me and not the pretend me and not the me that fits in anybody's box. The funny thing about it is, that is the mission statement of this church is to grow to be who you really are, wow.

Hopefully tomorrow I will be able to call Troy to see what he can tell me about that area and how he can help me with housing. For this, I would be willing to go to school, to learn more about God's word, whew. What is going on?

July 1, 2007—Sunday—9:42pm

I made it through another day. I feel my load getting a little lighter. Today a lady bought my sofa and wouldn't you know she was referred to Craigslist yesterday at the same time that I posted the items. God sent her to me and she is a therapist that works with battered women. Wow! I guess I sowed into her ministry which was a part of my past. That is a sofa that women will sit on who are trying to be healed. I know the energy in the sofa will help them. Wow! What a thing to happen. It's like my life has come full circle.

I gave the baby's stuff away today and of course that was energetically freeing. I am finally moving forward. I feel like things are finally coming together.

Today I talked to Troy about the possibility of being a youth pastor in Cleveland and his response was, it would be right up my alley. There was no delay before making that response and he's not that type of person. He is pretty square in that his responses are generally genuine. He doesn't put a lot in to trying to impress or being phony, especially with me. We tend to have a pretty open relationship in that we tell as much truth as possible. As I think about it more, I think of the words I spoke to Constance. Do for a career what you would do anyway. I would talk to kids and try to lead them to Jesus for free. That is my natural self. When I think of what Joyce says about how she could stand and talk all night, I can see myself standing in front of a group of youth just talking and talking and never being at a loss for words. I would be able to keep their attention too because that's what I'm good at and I think I would be even better with the freedom of being my true self. I can see myself working with the parents because that's what I'm used to. I would also like to do mentoring because I can see myself encouraging and not appearing to know it all. God truly stands near me because I can feel His presence often when I am connected to Him. I also think of the conversation with Constance about finding out who you are. This was interesting because that is the mission statement of the church and that is my main focus with young people. I am going to think about this a little more. I mean, listen to God. Then I am thinking of calling the church and asking if the position is still available and finding out more about the church. Actually, I think I will just ask about the church anonymously and see what happens. It just came to mind that I should take the path of least resistance and depending on the response I might just take steps to make this happen. Again, if this falls into place it is a sign to follow the trail.

July 4, 2007—Wednesday—12:57am

Yesterday I applied for a job that I believe God wants me to have. I am having to be patient with everything I am trying to do right now, but I know that it will all work out better than I could have imagined. Things are going to be great.

July 10, 2007—Tuesday—3:30am

The youth nights at the church keep coming up in my mind. I really regret not having a better attitude about serving. But I do know I did the best I could. There were some definite situations where I handled them to the best of my ability. I think maybe what is really bothering me is I spoke bad things about someone else, but more importantly I wish things could have been different. For all the years I have been in recovery I haven't had a situation to plague me the way this has. Maybe it's because it's about God and He is ultimately important to me.

I think a part of it is I expected more from people who are believers. I expected acceptance, understanding, and maybe even love—because I know I am a true Christ follower and I thought that should have been enough. But in my heart of hearts, I think this strain was about me not getting on board with his program and my instructions from God were not to do that. Pastor William even understood. This is what I think this whole conflict was about and he also saw me as a threat—because I knew the students more intimately than he did and I didn't need him for anything.

I was there on an assignment from God and I did as I was

instructed by God. I just wish things had turned out better and I wish he would teach the kids things they can use. To be honest, I think he is taking advantage of his position of power. Because I think it should have been clear to him that I was there for the kids and he should have been more supportive of me. I'm angry because I expected more from a person of God. I know that I'm a person of God, but he has studied and everything which I feel makes him more official. I am trying not to judge him, but I think he's not a true Christian. I think he might even have some problems with race. I am so disappointed. I really did open up. And him and his phony wife just walked in and hurt me.

July 12, 2007—Thursday—4:48am

What a night I had. I located a friend of mothers and I read and re-read Alan's old love letters. The hand of God is really working in my life. I feel the power of something great happening in my life.

It is not possible for me to find that woman's name and address in mother's things and it is definitely not possible for there to be a big ol' picture of her posted on the internet. And how weird is it that she's a teacher and teaches psychology. I know God has a special reason for me to speak with her and I can't wait to find out what it is.

Alan is just blowing my mind. When I read those letters, they detail the passion of our relationship that I thought could have only been in my mind. All of the letters were about him loving me and it was real. I am doing my best to follow God, but I feel the least I can do for Alan is to say that I am sorry. Because if he loved me half as much as those letters stated then he has to still remember that pain. I know that old hurts are not necessarily forgotten or healed. I don't know why I ran into him and then couldn't speak with him, but I believe that right now I owe him an apology.

July 14, 2007—Saturday—2:53am

Yesterday was a very interesting day. I cried a lot and talked to

Alan. I didn't talk to him in person, I talked to him in the spirit. I have come to the realization that he feels the same way I do. If he was mad at me ten years after we broke up stating that I cheated on him that means he remembers and he still feels it. If he remembers and feels it, he really feels it. That means the good also. I think when I saw him that day he was ready to give me a chance, but that one problem caused him to get scared. He was kind to me on the phone when I called to give him the right number, but I think he went through the same anxiety that I did waiting for him to call. He really wanted to talk to me and he was anxious, but when he couldn't he was really disappointed. I think that incident scared him because it probably brought up a lot of old feelings about how he felt about me, good and bad. He probably questions if he can do this again.

I know he still loves me because when I told him I would be leaving soon he sounded disappointed by the drop in his voice. What I know for sure is what happens between a man and a woman is personal. Only Alan and myself know what's really going on between us. Just like with Bishop. We had fallen in love instantly. I know my Alan is going through the same thing I am. He's thinking about if he should call or not because of what he has to lose. I know that deep burning passion is still in him— because if he had it at twenty something, at forty something I know there is no limit. Alan at that time had enough passion to blow the roof off. I don't mean sexual. I mean intensity. His words in his letters were soul stirring. You could feel every word. His writing has the passion that mine has today. It's sincere and original. If he had all of that then, I can only imagine what kind of love he could give today. He is the man I want right now. The kind of man he was then.

My relationship with him is the one regret I can think of in my life. I wish I had never hurt him. Most other things in life I accept and say they have made me who I am today. But I do regret what happened with Alan. We were two young people trying to grow up. While going through my things today I found loan information for him from back in 1986. In 1986, I was two years out of high school and looking at the things I found in my mother's papers, things were pretty bad. She was sick and didn't have a lot of money and I didn't help. I was having problems with trying to grow up and he was trying to figure out what he wanted to do with his life and his family wanted him to hurry up. We were both very young and it was the wrong time.

I feel if we gave it a go right now it would be perfect. I believe the guy he was then is the guy I'm looking for now with up to date changes of a mature forty something year old man. The biggest catch is if he's a Christian, but if he isn't he may be ready to give God a chance.

On the day we saw each other it was supposed to happen. I was supposed to meet the guy at the store and give him my number and invite him to church and change my number so he couldn't reach me and go downtown and meet Alan. And I was supposed to not speak with him after that time.

Twenty years ago when we dated we were in the same place of trying to figure out life and now we're in the same place of waiting to be fulfilled. I know he's thinking about me like I'm thinking about him. And he's probably wondering what to do just like I'm wondering what to do. I can feel Alan. What a treasure it would be to have a good man by my side. I would marry him tomorrow. It does hurt to long for him, but it does feel good to lie here and let my feelings for him soak in. I love Alan. After all of these years—he is the one that got away. The one that I pursued every time I saw him. I never stopped loving him. I am allowing myself to feel these feelings. It's not sexual. It's love. It's in my heart.

July 16, 2007—Monday—1:41am

Wow! When I got up out of bed yesterday morning and thought I was going to write a letter to Alan I was stopped cold in my tracks. I checked in with God to see what information I would get. And lo and behold Joyce told me that God told Abraham to leave his family and his father's house and she said to the audience, but he didn't tell him to take his nephew, Lot. What she said to the audience is that when you leave don't take anyone from your past with you like Abraham did because that was what

Lot represented. And when Abraham got to where he was going he ended up having strife with Lot so he was distracted from what God was asking him to do.

That put a stop to me writing the letter to Alan because that's telling me that he definitely would have gone with me if I had asked.

Well, Sunday evening I was led to run some errands and who did I see after I pulled out of the car wash? If I had gone after I got my clothes out of the dryer, I would have missed him. I saw Tony. I knew him from the back of his head. He then turned to the side and there is not another profile like his. It was him. I had to do this anyway, but I went to the light and went down a street and turned back around. I pulled up in the laundromat right behind him. It was so unbelievable. He kneeled down at my window, but kept his glasses on so I couldn't gaze into his eyes. He was so hyper and I was really laid back. There is something he still doesn't know because he was asking me questions the way he used to. I asked him if he got married the weekend of September 11, and he said yes. He asked me if that incident was a sign that he should not have gotten married. In response, I made a face, but didn't say anything.

He asked me what I was doing and I told him I had been teaching English for the past four years and he seemed really surprised. He was really surprised that I was in Berkeley. I'm sure this means I have been right under his nose for all of this time because he lives right down the street from me.

I was really calm about seeing him. He said, "Aren't you going to ask me how I'm doing?" I said, "Oh yes, how are you doing?" He said that his wife wants to leave him and go back to Tanzania and that marriage sucks. He also said his daughter is in Kentucky. I felt a sense of sadness from him. Maybe he was looking at me and thinking he made the wrong decision because he ended up being with someone who is hurting him and I never did that to him. I only loved him and he took me for granted and ran from me like the plague. As he can see, things turned out pretty good for me. I made it clear that I'm looking for a

Christian school and I am free to travel the world. He could have been with me. I feel bad for him because I'm sure he knows he could have had a better life with me.

He complimented me on my car and said, "Wow, this is nice." He was driving a car that looked okay, but had a hanger for an antenna. I feel sorry for him. I am going to sit and talk with him when I get a chance to really find out how far he has come and if he has learned anything in the last ten years. He was twenty-five, now he's at least thirty-five. I want to know that he has learned something because I do care about him. I will impart to him any last words of wisdom with hopes of helping him in his future. I also want to know what happened to his family and how they are doing.

I believe this is a test I will pass because I will not be distracted by continuing to talk to him or have an affair with him. This is my way of moving into my new life in a good way. The way we left things could have been better. He is very anxious to talk to me because he openly wanted to exchange numbers. He didn't just make it one way. He is open to talking with me. I think it's good to be able to face things instead of running away. More importantly, if you care about someone, it's good to let them know and to find out if they are okay and if you can help. It's what Jesus would do.

Also he happens to be working in the same city that my work assignment is in. This is the same company that gave me a job after I let him go so that he could get married. This same company is giving me a job now and I will let him go again. I think this is a sign that I'm exactly where I'm supposed to be.

July 17, 2007—Tuesday—1:06am

Yesterday was the first day on my new assignment and I made it. Even though the training was a bit trying. I held my patience. At some point I looked into the trainer's face and said, "Lord help me." I know God helped me in that moment, but I think it might also have helped me to understand what I was feeling and to be more patient with myself. After all of what happened today, after reflecting, I noticed I wasn't able to think of a lot of bad things about my trainer the way I usually would. I would usually look to find something wrong with a person or to judge them about something.

I can see that God is moving more into my life because I was not able to do that. He is taking over my thinking and I am glad because that's most of the battle. Everything starts with a thought and then moves into an action.

I also noticed I was able to talk to a complete stranger in the dentist's office about the person I used to be. There was a time when I would have been too ashamed to admit I had ever been anything less than what I am now. But I guess I can see and I really know that was another life. It's not me anymore and to share that with people is a testimony about what God can do. I don't believe this is all happening in my life. The major problems I was having are going away. I am doing better with my love walk by not judging and being more open.

I would have to attribute this to the fact that I'm doing nothing but spending time with God. I am no longer watching TV.

While I was on my job today I got a clear message about Indonesia. It just showed up on the computer screen—Indonesia. This is God telling me I should apply for the job there. What I'm getting from this experience is—there are different places I might be able to do the work He is calling me to do, but I need to be open to going wherever that is. That is how the Biblical story of Abraham relates to me... I'm being told to go but not where to go to. But I'll know when it's time to go. I believe I should apply for any job that suits the purpose of me teaching or working with kids in a way that helps them or teaches them to have a better life. I am getting closer and closer. I just need to be ready when it comes.

July 23, 2007—Monday—8:16pm

Right now I am walking around in a bit of a fog because of my reveling at all of the great things God is doing in my life. I have had now a total of three visits to the Holiday Clinic and all of them have been free. These first two visits were allowed based on a pending status because I was applying for health insurance. After I was denied I called later to find out what my status was because I still needed my final rabies shot. They told me it would cost $150 for a deposit and I would be billed for the rest. Today I arrived and again was in a bit of a fog. I registered and had a seat and realized they had not charged me the $150 deposit. I wondered if I should correct the young man who helped me, but I then realized it was not a mistake. Someone had done something to make that visit free. I know this because he did look me up in the computer and it should have given him information about my coverage. This was not a mistake. The visit was free. As I sat there stupefied all I kept thinking to myself is God pays for what He orders. This is what I kept hearing Joyce Meyer say in my head. This really freaks me out.

Then while I was sitting there an older Filipino man started talking to me about Christianity. I told him for sure that I am one and that is why I'm here to get shots to travel and do God's work. The man named Chico gave me a gospel track and told me I should talk to the pastor of his church because they give away a lot of money to people working as a missionary. His church could be a source of money for my trip.

I talked to the gentleman about the Peace Corps because he mentioned it to me and we came to the conclusion that it was not a good fit because their mission was different. I need to go with an organization that is going with the intention of sharing God's love. People need to know that anything good that is done for them is because of God's love. They also need to be brought to Christ.

Yesterday in church the pastor talked about the missionary families and how proud he was to see people so committed. He knows I was really hearing his message and he mentioned again that the church has taken care of a particular family for at least 20 years. He did say to not let fear be the reason for not going. He helped with the idea about what to do with mother's jewelry and that was to sell it. He read that Scripture again about the rich young ruler who was to sell his things and follow the Lord. He kept saying, "If you are here today hearing this message and it relates to you then it is meant for you because it was written some time ago." That sermon validated my thoughts also because I think my mother would want me to sell her things to get the money to travel because giving it to Cissy is not the answer. I think Cissy may be a bit put off because I did mention giving the jewelry to her, but I didn't. I know she is aware that happened.

July 24, 2007—Tuesday—11:25pm

I have been in a funky mood all day. At this time in the evening, I'm realizing that it must be because I have started taking my medication again. God showed up again when I went to get a copy of my shot record. A young lady found that I still needed two more shots and she gave me one of them today. This was free of charge. But I know better. In a couple of days I will check in with the billing department and tell them I had the shot and ask if I owe them money. My attitude has to be because of my medication because I don't know the last time I've felt this funky even when things were going terribly.

Tonight Eloise called me and I hate that I answered the phone. She has nothing to talk about. She talked about her hurting arm, but is it just because she's not taking care of herself? I just know I want to take care of myself and have a full life so when I'm older I can look back and know I never missed any opportunities in life. I was already feeling bad, then started feeling better—but after talking to her I realized the conversation was a waste of my time. She didn't have anything relevant to say about her life and it made no sense to talk about mine. I know what I'm doing. Why should I take the time to tell someone else? Is it maybe because she cares or is she just bored with her own life? I am so angry with myself for wasting my time. She bores me silly and when I talk to her there are always these distractions and it gets on my nerves. She won't be talking to me again for a while and I mean that!! It's a waste of my time.

July 26, 2007—Thursday—12:35am

I am feeling a bit of stress because I am still waiting for my passport. I had a dream that God was telling me to apply for another one, but when I called to make an appointment to get one they said I had to have a travel itinerary or a job offer letter from an employer. This confirms for me that I can not be dishonest no matter what the circumstances. I did learn that if I do get an offer before my passport shows up there is a way to get one. That is a big relief. I am still left with not knowing what God wants me to do. Does He want me to go to some random place and just apply for another passport or just wait for the one that I've applied for? Maybe He's just telling me that it's just going to take the time that it's going to take. Just like when I was waiting for the baby. I believe He waited until I was truly ready. I had everything I needed and I had done everything He had asked me to do—even quit my job. That was the thing I believe that really made it happen because I was then free.

I think the light just came on in my head. It's not about the passport. It's about me. I have to get rid of what's in the way which is all of my stuff. I have to continue to get rid of my jewelry and my mother's furniture and then I will have freed up enough space in my heart making me ready for something new.

You have to close one door before another one will open. I can't really be ready for my new life if I'm still holding on to things from my past. On Tuesday when I was trying to rush through the papers of my past, I became overwhelmed because those were things that it took me years to accumulate. I felt a feeling of peace when I looked at them slowly because I was acknowledging the life I had and I was saying good-bye to it. When I shredded each piece of paper it was good-bye. It was more meaningful. If I had only put them in the trash it wouldn't have had the same impact.

When Mo Mo came into my life I looked at those things and put them away for a time when I would need them again, but now they must go for good. I don't need them anymore. As I keep telling myself, where I'm going I won't need them. I must know that this process is going to take as long as it takes and I will wait patiently for God.

I have truly risen to a new level with God because He wants me pure. He now has required me to not take any medications. I know this for a fact because after I had my first series of vaccinations, I could not take my thyroid medication because I got sick as a dog. On Monday I had my last rabies shot and on Tuesday I had a tetanus shot. On Monday night and Tuesday night I took my thyroid medicine and by Wednesday I was sick as a dog. I was laid out with an upset stomach and I slept the whole day to try and sleep off those drugs.

When I was still watching TV I can remember watching a program that mentioned how your body can reject things that are not good for it. I can remember an adjustment period when I first started taking the medication and how that affected my moods, but I don't remember getting sick. Sick is a sign of poisoning. That medication acts like poison for my system. I am truly at a higher level with God. He wants to make sure I am at my purest self so He may reach me. I can do this. In the past few weeks that I haven't had the medication, I have had my strongest days as a Christian. One of my darkest was the day after I took the medication. I am having to go back to people and apologize for my behavior that was nasty and out of control.

Even though I had plans today to go out and sell jewelry, I think God gave me a chance to get all of this in perspective. He is giving me a chance for this stuff to cool off before He sends me out on another job.

Now that I believe I have agreed to accept help for my journey, I have to decide when I'm going to speak with Pastor William. There is a part of me that says to wait until I have finished getting rid of stuff.

July 28, 2007—Saturday—1:24am

This latest assignment from God is not at all funny. I now only work and was almost in tears because I am not able to do the things I have done for most of my life, which is turn on the TV. The TV was my best friend and confidant. I guess God has taken it away from me because I did give it more time than I gave to Him.

All I can do now is sit in this apartment and spend time with Him. It makes me feel that He loves me more than He loves other people because He is demanding more of my time than He is from other people. It also validates the call on my life is serious because these are serious conditions He is asking me to live in. He needs my full attention and my only interaction with the world should be a necessity or to be a blessing to someone. The funny thing about all of this is I know for sure I'm not allowed to watch TV.

He probably tried this before when He broke both TV's in the house and my home computer and my work computer. But I was just not having it. Just like the TV repairman said, just like everything went out they all came back into function at the same time.

Before I started taking my medication again, I was almost in a constant meditative state. It did feel good to be that close to God.

God has always done things for a reason and I really believe this new lifestyle is really for the purpose of preparing me for a change that is about to come. God had asked me to give up lots of things along the way, but I have to admit it has always worked to my benefit and it has always been easy.

When I gave up sugar and other noisy foods it helped my mental state as well as my health. I stopped having gas. When He asked me to give up cigarettes my teeth whitened and when I gave up alcohol that was one less thing to hide or be ashamed of. It also helped me to grow more in Christ because I didn't have crutches anymore. When I gave up men it helped me to get more control of my life. Decisions I made because of relationships with men created emotional turmoil in my life. I also had to worry about my health because I was still having sex. Even when God asked me to give up my job there was a life changing experience right around the corner.

God has continued to prune away the things in my life that were not needed. As a result, I grew closer to Him. The latest of these is the medication. Giving up the medication has brought me closer to God because I can feel Him better and I'm more relaxed.

It would be nice to know where I'm going so I can tell people for sure. Is it really Africa?

July 28, 2007—Saturday—6:58am

I had been up reading my Bible when I realized I kept having interruptions from outside thoughts. When I finally decided to put down my Bible and listen to these thoughts I was having I realized it was all about me and my stuff. I was thinking I wished I had sister-in-laws I could trust with some things. Then I referred back to the necklace I gave Peaches that she still has not called me to thank me for. This allows the devil to make me think I can't trust her mother.

I have things I don't want to sell and I don't want to give them away, but I am feeling led to get rid of them. I felt so frustrated that I got up and took the shower I needed to try to wash some of that confusion down the drain.

While in the shower a tear rolled down my cheek as I became overwhelmed by the fact that I have been given this assignment by God which is huge for me. I think it didn't really hit me until now. I have heard the message at least four or five times now about the rich young ruler and how he is asked to sell all of his things to follow God. This is one of the most painful things I have ever had to do. I guess the sentiment is that some of the things were given to me and I would like to give the items back. But I want the items returned to me when I come back to the states. Even though I don't know if I'll be returning, some of the items are things that can't be returned because the person is deceased or no longer in my life.

I guess this is why this process is going to take the time it's going to take. Maybe it is helpful that we are going into the cycle of the full moon on Monday to get rid of things. I can see why I'm not allowed to watch TV because I need all of my attention available to handle this project.

This is my wilderness and I shall not complain, but I have called on God to help me to do this thing He has asked of me. As I mentioned earlier, everything He has asked me to do has brought me to a better place, even when I had to give up my teeth. Now I have straighter teeth with fresher breath. I have learned that the wilderness is for the purpose of humbling and the testing our faith in God. Can you trust Him to work this for your good? With many of my things, even my clothes, I see them as things I can get again. It's the small things like jewelry that is really putting me to the test.

What I know for sure—is I have done everything God has asked me to do and I'm sure I will manage this as well. This process of giving up stuff is actually giving me a headache. :(I think it's making my chest hurt too.

July 29, 2007—Sunday—1:51am

I really had a weird day yesterday. I finally called Alexis and she told me she was just getting out of the hospital for dehydration and complications with her diabetes. She said all of this happened because she was on the Beyonce' diet of eating only once a day. I was totally in shock when she told me this because I couldn't imagine anything crazier until she told me she had planned to go on an internship in Spain, I think for a year. I believe she hasn't even been married for a year. She says that I inspired her.

When I told her I was going to Africa the first thing out of her mouth was, I'm jealous. When I went to see her, she was not joking. She was twice the size of what she had been. She must be out of her mind to pull these kinds of stunts. She is too old to be starving herself and that is crazy to leave your new husband.

The truth is she only married him because she was miserable and thought she couldn't do any better. Now the drastic weight loss attempt was only because I have not gained weight. Do I have to leave her alone completely because she is insane? I am astonished at how quickly she could flip out and make such crazy decisions. I guess I'm judging, but I think I'm right on this one. She still has not given up on competing with me. That is not good for a relationship. That is what made me truly disconnect from Alejandra. Jealousy is dangerous. It can be nice sometimes, but it can also burn you.

The next weird thing that happened today was that I talked to Eloise and I think our wires got a bit crossed. She thought I wanted her advice on my life and my decisions about traveling. Because I am working on my listening skills, I sat and listened to everything she had to say. She even went back as far as Mo Mo and what she thought about that. If I was not a Christian woman, I could have really hurt her feelings—because she is sitting in a house she has been in for forty years with the same man and a rotten child. I don't think she has ever taken a risk in her life other than with her hair.

I thank God for the mother that He gave me because she really understood me. She was all about me being my own person and making my own mistakes. That is what parents are supposed to do and my mother did that for me. She let me grow. She let me find my own strength. Just like Joyce says, don't ask other people what to do because they don't know what they're doing themselves. They are over there praying that boy through high school and I have graduated from college twice without the help of any parents. So how dare she think her words would make much sense in my world? She can't imagine the life I'm living—because she has never been free. She has never even lived on her own. And I dare to think also that she could even imagine what it means to love God so much that you would do anything for Him. And on top of that, God loves me and anything I do for Him will be for my own good.

She doesn't even know God the way I do. Until recently, she has really only had the same job. It would have been more polite to consider all of these things before she opened her mouth to a forty-one year old woman who she has no obligation to. That means her words are meaningless.

I guess it angers me so for a person to be so bold with their views about someone else's life that they really have nothing to do with. She could have kept all of that to herself because she didn't even know what she was talking about. To get into some parts of Africa you have to show proof of means. I have references of people who live there so I would not just show up. She doesn't even know if that's where I'm going. The whole thing was ridiculous and I am very tempted to call her and let her know how I feel about it. She was out of line—because really what I do is none of her business. When you get right down to it. She pays for nothing in my life and even when I borrowed luggage from them it was some old oily bag. She didn't loan me one of her nice pieces of luggage which would have made me look like a decent human being in the airport. I would not have had to carry that big bag on my shoulder either. Does she really think in her mind that they have done so much for me? That is why I never slip and call her mother—because she doesn't love me like a mother. She makes me feel like they made me feel as a child. They make you feel uncomfortable when you get anything from them. What I will do is give them back that cooker so I don't have to feel like they did that for me. She doesn't even know that's why I don't eat a morsel of food at their house—because they make you feel it. They offer it, but they make you feel guilty for taking it. They are not as generous and giving and loving as they think they are. That is why even though I grew up the way I did, I'm glad because I knew my mother loved me and if she could have done better for me she would have. She did her best for me and us kids. She kept us all together as long as she could. She had offers along the way from different people that wanted us, but she made the right decision to keep us.

I'm glad that I had my mother. She was a strong woman and I am respecting her even more as I grow older. I am glad I am living a life that she would be proud of.

She really let it fly. It was like she was saying that I'm stupid. That is was ridiculous for me to think I could have kept that baby and it is ridiculous for me to think this mission of mine is going to work. I think I might be done with her. As soon as I can, I will drive over there and take her that pot and talk to my Godfather and Jonathan and be done with it. I also need to consider changing my life insurance. I know underneath everything she's a nice person with a good heart, but I don't think it's good for me to have relationships with people who don't get me at this stage of the game. I am too old to keep explaining myself to people. I won't even chalk this up to caring because Carrie gets me and I have always felt an openness from her even when I was a child. Carrie gets that I am smart enough to make my own decisions and I will do what is right for me. The place I'm at in my life right now is a gift and I should take advantage of this opportunity. Carrie is a genuine person. You generally know where she's coming from.

I believe I have given them all I want to give them and I don't care to see how their story ends. Not understanding me at this stage in my life is not an option. She really let loose and told me what she thought. How could I think that baby was going to be with me? In the back of her mind, I heard her say, stupid.

July 29, 2007—Sunday—5:14am

After all of that rambling and talking in the mirror and stuff, I have come to realize it is best to end the relationship with my Godparents. I know for sure my Godmother does not understand me and I can probably also say she doesn't respect me either—because she breaks my rules. She calls my house when I ask her not to. This is a sign of disrespect because she is aware of what she's doing. She has to say to herself she is going to do it anyway. That is a person that does not respect my boundaries and they don't work for her. That means the relationship does not work—because I am not going to make that adjustment for her. That too is the reason why she doesn't know where I live. She would just show up whenever she wanted to. I have decided I am going to be woman enough to tell her to her face. That way I don't have to deal with it later. Just get it over with. After thinking about it, she would be the only person breaking that rule if I had a phone while out of the country. Even Bobby gets my drift on that. He's not a total knuckle head.

I have talked to God about this and I have not received any nudges telling me my thoughts are off. I know she loves me, but the relationship is not working. It takes more than love to make a relationship work. It also takes respect and understanding and it's not there. I feel like this is a load off my back. That way I can stop trying to pretend they are something to me they're not. It's better to just not have them in my life at all. They are nothing like my birth parents and my father was absent and my mother was ill and poor. But I know in my heart they gave me what they could. If my father had a pot of money while he was living, he would have done anything possible for me and the same for my mother.

I know it's good to be grateful, but I feel like a relationship with them I can just do without because I feel the lack. Even my crazy cousin doesn't give me the feeling of lack. He would always do what he could for me even if his motives were skewed. The same for my aunt. It's like when a person always has a limit on what they will do for you. Or if there is an item that you need—they will never give you the best one or better yet you're not worthy of it.

I know that's not the case for Jonathan. I know Darrell buys the best for him. I guess that's a part of it too. They make me feel not good enough to be given certain things. I'm not good enough the way I am because I'm not the way they want me to be.

I'm totally different.

I don't think it's healthy to be in a relationship with people who play the role of your parents who make you feel that you're not good enough.

There is no one else that I can think of off the top of my head that makes me feel that way. Even my aunt, she may not like the way I am, but she still knows I'm hers and she makes me feel like she would give me the best of anything and that I'm worthy.

Even Conrad and Carrie make me feel good enough. My brother Caleb is questionable.

August 2, 2007—Thursday— 4:27am

Yesterday was a wow day. I got up at the last minute and rushed to meet Pastor William to discuss my future. I so looked forward to this meeting because I believed he would be telling me the destination I was to meet. I sat and talked with him and shared with him my admiration for him because of his commitment to God.

After we covered all of that I finally got to the mission stuff which included all of the work I have done to prepare for my assignment. He was glad to hear about the miracles God has performed in my life and said, just like God has shown me those miracles, there may be others to come. This led him to tell me about the MAPS program for missionaries. This is the one I told him I don't qualify for because you can't have more than $100 worth of debt. This is why he again said I could get a miracle for this debt like I did for the other.

Before I left he prayed for me that God would show me where I'm supposed to go. I stayed there for a good while after that and talked to my good friend Zena. I caught her up on everything and just like I shared with her is what I know for sure. God wants to use my voice. He is now preparing me by filling me with the Word and continuing to build my character and working with me on my mouth. He needs for my character to be strengthened because that will be reflected in what I say.

When I was about to leave, a man came to the church and needed directions to the Safe Place. I took it upon myself to guide him down there by him following me in my car even though my gas hand was on E. After we got there, we stood outside of the place and talked a bit and I knew this was an opportunity for me to help. My rent was due on that day, but I didn't have all of the money and his goal was to go back to Arizona to a job and a place to stay. We talked for a good while then we hit the road. We went to my regular gas station then to say good-bye to his stepfather. Afterwards we went to McDonald's then the dollar store. I realized even though he said he just needed gas money, I knew he would need food for the kids along the way. I bought Vienna sausages, crackers, fruit bars, water, candy and pudding for the trip. Then we went to my bank then to Super Foods to get fruit the kids requested like grapes, apples and bananas. I also realized that in his state I should finish up the job so that nothing was left to chance. I bought plastic forks, spoons and napkins. Now my job was complete. Of the $100 that I had taken out of the bank the items were just under $20. So I gave him the remaining $80 and one dollar for the new purse I bought for his daughter from the dollar store. I also gave a few coins to his son. Now everything was done.

I then talked to Lance for a bit to share some words of wisdom. I also asked his daughter to help him out along this journey by being good and being grateful that he was doing the best he could.

I left that family not knowing what their future would be like, but I knew for sure that I was supposed to meet and help them on that day. I questioned myself later about my current circumstances about not having the money for my rent. I realized all of the decisions I had made up to that moment were supposed to happen. If not, I would not have been there to exercise my faith in God and give so willingly to those less fortunate—when I was so much in need myself.

If I had any less faith I could not have done it because all I would have been thinking about was as Joyce says, "What about me? What about me? What about me?" in the robot voice. But as she also says, I was already over my head in need so if God could provide one amount for my rent He could cover a little more. This is what I believe. So the discontinued temp assignment, which led me to the Indonesia job and the passed up security job, that just didn't feel right, were all right decisions.

I did say I had a strong feeling that I was to not leave this apartment, but is it time to go now? I have until the leasing office opens to find out if this is what God wants me to do.

I also have some time before I can call Trinity church. Pastor William said yesterday it is not determined and that helped me because it took the pressure off of me about going to Africa. I am to go wherever God leads me and I can't explain it, but that Trinity church is screaming at me. Even after Pastor William prayed for me, I still kept getting that message. The funny thing about it is I had every intention to call yesterday but couldn't because of my project with Lance. When I look at where God is leading me with my talents and how He wants to use me it really is the ministry. If this is the gift and God is giving it to me—I am happy already. Or I can at least say thank you because I know that whatever it is it's going to be just for me. I'm so happy for me.

August 4, 2007—Saturday—6:55pm

How do I know God loves me? Because He didn't allow my mother to give me away to anyone when she had the opportunity. Because He kept her alive until a time in my life when I was ready for her to go—I could then live without her. He didn't take her when I was a child. He kept me from getting hooked on drugs even though I tried some of the most dangerous and addictive stuff. He kept me alive even though I risked my life numerous times with strangers, men and just bad circumstances. Sometimes even with a gun being put to my head on more than one occasion. And an obvious situation where my ex-husband could have beaten me to death—had God not gotten me out of there. I know with all of my heart that he probably came by that apartment when I was moving out, but I had probably just missed him. And as diligently as he looked for me he could not find me. If I can recall correctly he even went to Cynthia's house and I had never even taken him there before, so he was really looking. But God put His cover of protection over me to keep me safe. I have since even lived a public life of teaching and still been safe. God allowed that child to not be born because I would have had a lifetime connection with him and his family. That seed could not live in my body and even the process of getting rid of it was so painful that it was crippling. God worked all of that out in my favor. It was probably because of all of the sexual abuse that kept the pregnancy from coming to be. My body is a temple for God and his tainted seed could not live in God's house. It had to be destroyed. That child was not to come from my body and see the light of day.

August 7, 2007—Tuesday—3:33am

Now I remember what has been holding up my progress with moving things out of this house. Earlier I was going through a small stack of papers which I thought were harmless enough, when lo and behold there it was. The gripping evidence from my past that told me that the same flaws I have today, I had twenty years ago. That is devastating.

It's even more hurtful to realize the pain that I have caused someone in the process. I hadn't realized I had been a Diva for so long. I guess I know that there has always been so much hurt and pain underneath it all. I guess I'm really not the same because when I was faced with the guilt of hurting someone, it sent me to bed. And that is what happened the last time. I can remember saying to myself that I couldn't deal with it and went to bed and didn't touch any papers for weeks. I know that I'm not the same just from a few months ago. I looked at most of the same stuff before Mo Mo came and I wasn't overcome with anything that I can remember. Now I'm a different person and I truly care about how I affect people. I apologize even for the slightest thing and that's why I outed myself about not being nice and apologized to Alisha because I felt guilty. I think that might have put a damper on things with us, but I was too concerned with her finding out from someone else. I know I'm not perfect, so the least I can do is apologize to someone if I'm not all that I should be.

I know there are no accidents and while looking through those papers, I realized today is Tyler's birthday. I feel led to contact him and wish him a happy birthday and apologize. I will wait and listen to God, but I don't think there's anything wrong with an apology. The others that I have run into I know it was for the purpose of witnessing to them that I am now saved. This would be the same thing with Tyler. It is coming to mind to not let fear stand in my way. Another way of saying it is don't be guided by fear.

August 8, 2007—Wednesday—12:02am

What I know for sure is if you love someone you never stop. When you see that person the feelings come rushing back. But you then have to make a decision as to what you're going to do next and how a relationship with that person might impact your current life and theirs as well.

I loved Tyler and he loved me and seeing him yesterday brought back a lot of feelings. I can tell that he still loves me because it's always in the eyes. When he first realized it was me, he had to grab hold of the railing in front of him and drop his head and take a deep breath. I thought he was either going to faint or cry. I think tears actually came to his eyes. It wasn't fear or pain that he remembered. It was like someone had kicked him in the stomach. He was in shock. He truly loved me and it was all over his face.

He is now a full grown man of 42 on yesterday, but I could still see the Tyler that I loved. Even though the years have shown him many things, his heart still belonged to me. I regret that he probably fell in love with me all over again. I also know that he recognized that I'm a better person then I was back when we were together. He realized that I repeated over and over again that I was sorry and I appreciated him being there for me when I really needed him.

He heard me. He got it. And even though in the days of the past we celebrated birthdays with lots of gifts and all of the trimmings, I know this may have been one of his best birthdays ever. Because he received an apology and thank you all on the same day. What I know for sure is it was a gift of love from my heart. He knows I had to have loved him for me to come back after all these years and thank him for his love. He now knows that I got it and I know that had to make him feel like he was on top of the world to be so appreciated and understood. I know now that either of those things is precious, but for them to be all rolled up in one is special. It makes you feel like you can do anything—like walk on water.

I love Tyler and he will always have a special place in my heart, but I do know everything worked out the way it was supposed to. We were not supposed to be together, but there were qualities I should appreciate about him—so when they show up again in my life I will see them clearly. I will always love Tyler for being a man of his word. He was there when I needed him the most. That is an example of love. He made me feel special and he understood me and I think we even had the same love language—gifts.

He gave me things I asked for and even things I didn't. I knew for sure that I was loved. He even looked past my flaws like they didn't exist. He was really just tolerating them because he loved me.

I know he is good to his wife because he was good to me and he was young enough to not know better. She is a lucky woman. I kept asking him for hugs and while we were at my car in the street, I held on to him and lay in his chest because I didn't want to let go. I felt from him what I felt before—safety and love. I felt comfort and warmth and acceptance. And even though he has changed a bit physically it was clear to him I didn't care. I just wanted to hold on to someone I knew loved me.

He won't tell because he loves me and he doesn't want to see me hurt anymore. I know he will protect my heart from that. I have proven to him I love him despite anything I've done and for that I'm sure he's grateful. Everyone is glad to know they are loved, especially when you want it from a person. Even if it comes twenty years too late. Love is timeless. It goes on forever. As time goes by, the way it looks changes, but it still serves the same purpose of warmth and security and acceptance.

At some point he did ask if he could keep the papers that he had written to me, but after I drove away I came back and asked him if he wanted them and he said he couldn't because he's married. But I should keep them to remember him by. He knows that we won't be together, but he wants me to remember our love because it has never died. I didn't show up on his birthday with anything in a box, but I'm sure I left him with a shine on his heart. He knows beyond a shadow of a doubt he is loved and appreciated.

His request of me was to come by and see him sometimes. Even though I'm still working on my hearing, I heard that because he repeated it a few times. That's where it gets a bit sketchy. I know how we both feel and there is no way for us to see each other and not have a bunch of emotional stuff come up. Because love is in the heart and even though we don't look the same as we did twenty years ago, our hearts are still the same. The chemistry is still there and this is where I have to sow the seed of discipline because I would not want someone coming into my husband's life and tempting him. It might be okay to show up and do what I did yesterday, but anything more is risky. I will probably be able to stop by and sit with him before I leave and talk about what we didn't talk about. But visiting is out of the question. We love each other in spite of all the years and everything and spending time together would only stir things up like it did yesterday.

What I know for sure is the one thing people are often times willing to risk everything for is to be with someone they connect with—especially love. I have to admit it warms my heart greatly that he still loves me after all of these years. He said more than once to just come by and see him sometimes—like the old people say because their heart needs it—because you are such a source of joy for them, just your presence. He seemed okay and when I asked, he said things were great. But I can't even imagine what his life is like and knowing what I know now, he's very intelligent. So he would have to know what he's saying when he's asking me to visit him. He would have to know he would be looking at all of his feelings for me and the fact that I didn't turn out so bad.

What I know for sure is he is in my corner 100%. If I ever needed him, he would be there for me just like he was in the past—because he truly loves me.

I guess my tears are for the thoughts of having a good and true love in my life. That love I had was not perfect, but parts of it were. When I think about it he gave me the same look Alan did when I told him I was leaving. I didn't know forty would look like this. That you could look back twenty years and it would look like and feel like yesterday. I thought as you moved through life you would truly be leaving things in the past. But experience has shown me that it's all just a finger snap away. So it's important to make the days and the years good because you will never forget them. They will always be with you, a part of your spirit and all you have to do is push the right button to call them up. Therefore when you look back you will be looking at pretty pictures not scenes of shock, horror and disbelief. Live everyday as if it matters because it does. Your past can haunt you like a ghost in a scary movie so be careful of what kind of movies you're trying to make. Because they will be stored away on film as permanent record for later viewing for not just you but all. The movie is all about you and what you want to leave the world as a record of you. What kind of starring character are you?

What kind of movie are you currently working on? Is it a drama where that's all one would see because your life is so full of it? Or is it a family movie like a Hallmark movie? In those types of movies there may be some life challenges because that's real. But there's usually a message to the viewer about these challenges being in your life for the purpose of building strength and character. These movies also give examples about good ways to handle the situation. And there's always a happy ending because the main character never gave up on the goal.

This journey I'm on is truly an adventure. With all of the things I'm experiencing it's like I'm experiencing them in first and third person—because I always hear myself repeating to someone else what happened. I always have the experience of being in the middle of it and telling someone about it as a witness also. I know it's because I truly know someday I will tell my story. So while it's happening I'm always thinking of how I will explain it to someone else for their benefit.

God is using me right now because He has a purpose for my life and He wants me to do exactly what I'm doing—recording it to tell others. I prayed for favor everywhere I go and today I am living rent free in my apartment. God has His hand over me for protection. Today someone is going to pay me money for a lamp and it's the same money it's going to cost for my fingerprints. My horoscope even said for yesterday I would get a special parking space and see someone unexpectedly and catch a sale. I pulled up in a space that was where the reserved ones are in the garage and even the men walking by asked who I was to get such a privilege. I saw Henry Love unexpectedly and made sales on my items at home.

That trinity thing is still showing up. I am waiting to find out the true meaning of that. At this point it's a marker to show I'm on the right track. Yesterday after leaving Tyler while driving down San Pablo Avenue in Albany, I looked up and there was a sign on a business that said Trinity. I have driven down that street a many a time and how did I know to look up at that very moment? God is trying to tell me something. Even the other day I found the church in San Leandro that is on Trinity. This was after I was looking for youth ministries, but while looking on the website I realize they had just been to Malawi, West Africa. And again in that same evening while I was looking on websites as God instructed me, an SBA customer mentioned her employees went to Sierra Leone in West Africa to train the ladies on hair styling techniques. So West Africa seems to be on the table. I just have to stay on the trail to find out where to go.

My heart is at peace knowing I am truly following God's will for me. As long as I stay focused on that, everything will be fine. Like the man said in Mustafa's shop today, when the time is right everything will fall into place.

I'm so glad I went to see Tyler yesterday and I didn't let fear get in the way of that. He is truly aware of chemistry because he wouldn't even stand too close to me. Even after I commented on it he continued to move far away, but he says to come by and visit him sometime. I can remember now the one way he controlled me was with sex and he enjoyed that. He would kind of even torture me and ask me what my problem was and he knew it was him. I know who he's thinking about on the evening of his happy birthday. Again I say, if I wasn't a Christian woman... Tyler is one of the men who made love to me. I can still remember and I know he can too. It will be our little secret.

August 8, 2007—Wednesday—5:10pm

Another amazing day and I thank God for making me aware enough to see and appreciate it. I had a pretty sleepless night thinking of the events of yesterday. Something I needed to recall and record was again the odd story told by Carver at Mustafa's shop about his circumcision at age 22. He mentioned he was taken to Trinity hospital and that was also where he was born and his mother died. I have decided that it's critically important to my story to record all of my trinity sightings.

So in case I didn't mention it before, the day I was helping that family, the gas station was our first stop after I had determined it was for me to give them the money. There was a vehicle in front of me that said trinity on it. Today as I was coming home from checking my mail in Fremont there was a bus turning in front of my car telling me there were trinity condos available. That was something huge that I just couldn't miss. God is talking to me in this way because I don't even watch TV anymore, so He has to be creative to reach me. The funny thing is that it's working. I always tend to look up or in the direction I need to at the right time. I am very much on target and where God wants me to be.

Before I could leave the house today to get my fingerprints done which I realized would have cost me about $70, something told me to slow down and do things in a certain way. At the perfect time Olivia called and stopped me from getting the prints done because I didn't need them. It took everything in me to keep from telling her to have a blessed day. So instead I just said have a great one. In case I didn't mention it before, I was ministering to her in our interview yesterday and she knew it. She's smart enough to know what I was doing without saying God or Jesus once. She probably is even familiar enough with

Scripture to know which ones I was speaking from. God truly has a call on my life and like Joyce says, when the Holy Spirit hits you—you just want to share it with everybody, but you have to use wisdom.

I noticed Tyler had crosses all over his door yesterday. That is not the kind of thing that's an accident. He is a believer and he was an angel back then when he always came to my rescue. Where he's at right now even in that physical location is probably where he's supposed to be.

My heart is a bit heavy today and I am very quiet and thoughtful because of all that is going on. I saw Henry and I know it wasn't an accident. I conjured that up or God did should I say and thank God for helping me to be aware enough to see Him. I could have been turned with my back to him and he could have walked right on by. He could have gone out of the other side of the garage and that would have been it. But I listened to God and stood in the right place and caught him.

It is also amazing to see God cover my rent. Today is now the 8th of the month and I am still happily in my apartment with no interruption. Boy do I have a story to tell and I have to admit the Tyler thing still has me a bit shaken. So I've decided to put off the Alan apology until another time, if he doesn't call me first. I can't imagine having the whole conversation deal with Alan like I had with Tyler. That would be something to handle because just like when I saw him and waited all of that time for him to call—all of the feelings came rushing back to me. And what I know for sure is just what I went through with Tyler and I'm still feeling it today and probably will for a while, he is going to be going through the same thing. The heart never forgets. He will remember the pain, but the pleasure was so fulfilling. That's what stands out the most for him. That's why he said, come and visit me sometime. I have a secret place in his heart as he does in mine.

So all of the tears and praying I did when I saw Alan, I know he has also had the same feelings. I know he still is just like I am. He remembers me and he remembers the love. But he also knows I'm leaving and that was the face of a broken heart when I told him it would be soon. Just like Tyler saw I was different, Alan saw it too. And that I know was the something to really put a stir in his heart to make him want to scream. Alan is the threat because he probably does have no ties. No kids I mean. At least Tyler can't just up and go and Alan has the spirit of adventure that would make him say yes and follow the <u>love.</u> Even though I can't handle it now either, I think I should put off the call to Alan until I'm leaving for sure. I think it's a safe idea because if he's available the way I think he is—he could be a problem. He is sexy by my standards, clean, and smart. And I know the passion is still there. That's why I stepped back when he stepped toward me because he scared me. How could I handle any touch from him?

What I know for sure is God saved me from Bishop Davis. The difference between that situation with him and my husband is God. The fact that, no matter what, I never missed church. That saved me. My close and established relationship with God saved me because Bishop had the tools to reel me in. The sex was unstoppable and we had a special bond. We always knew what the other was thinking and feeling. We could feel each other from across town. I would have actually married him and repeated the same cycle of my previous marriage. And truth be told, I think I was pregnant with his baby. I have to admit I would like to see him to say goodbye—now that I'm prepared to see him with new teeth. I know he would be glad to see me, if he's not too embarrassed. He taught me that even after all that I've been through, I can still love and have an innocent and special connection with someone. I will always remember that first kiss and embrace. The night he took his daughter to the circus we kissed so intensely—that's when I think he asked me to marry him. The passion was so intense we both wanted to scream. I know it was pretty scary for him as well because he had just gotten out of a marriage. What we had was intense and sometimes beautiful. He will never forget me. I know I touched a place in his heart that was genuine. Just like he said, he hadn't felt like that for anyone since he was sixteen. He was the first one to say I love you because he thought I had said it first. He didn't feel comfortable saying it because it was so soon for us and he was even still legally married. When the song came on by Lionel Ritchie—I Call It Love, I can remember him lying in bed with his back to me and squeezing my hand. Because I knew him, I knew what that meant—that he did love me.

Bishop Wayne Davis, he was tough, smart, quick, confident, no-nonsense, sensitive, thoughtful, funny, compulsive, calculating, logical, confused, strong, complicated and had a swagger that would stop traffic.

I can remember when we met. We rode home from San Francisco State and we talked the whole way to Berkeley. We hit it off right away. He did ask me if I would go fishing with him, but because he had been married to a Gemini for twenty something years he understood my answer. We had an amazing day somehow functioning like husband and wife. We shopped and put the groceries away like a team. But I think it hit us both at the same time in the store when I called his name. Something happened immediately. He felt it and I did too. But before we could even get in the store, I stayed in the car to put on more lipstick just in case I saw kids or parents. He got out ahead of me and in his not very appealing black sweat suit, he got out and walked in the store. I said, "Who is he?" to myself. His physical appearance was very unassuming, but his walk told the story. It said I am all that and then some. And he sure was.

To lie on his chest was like a dream. To eat his food was enough to make you want to get fat. The non-stop sex was enough to make you want to have a baby. And his kisses would make you want to melt like butter. I did love Bishop, but like the e-mail says, as suddenly as he appeared it was that suddenly that he left. He knew I was about to end it. Just like Stephen said, he didn't want to hear it. He had already been dumped by his wife for the same reason—pills. Yet another relationship with great potential. We talked of performing at the Safe Place for Thanksgiving and that we could even start a foundation to help others. If he had been different, things could have been different. Bishop could not be alone and I know he missed me. We were also friends and we talked about my student Scott and the things he would do during the day. I hope God can heal his pain. My relationship with him very much resembled my relationship with my husband, but thank God it didn't get to the ugly part. So I can still love him in my heart.

I know despite my thoughts I may have, God will protect me. Because He has great plans for me. All I have to do is to continue to obey Him—no matter how small. The command of buying the ticket for Brooks is what got me to meet Bishop all those months later at that cancelled concert. I still believe that meeting was the will of God and Bishop's parting was the will of God also. He helped him to walk away, but I think we both needed that experience for our hearts because energetically we were at the same place of pain from past relationships. We both also needed to know it was possible to love again and that there was someone special still out there. We both got that. We both fell in love instantly and just like he said, he couldn't tell anybody because it sounded too crazy. We were both old enough to know what we had was special, but we both also knew it couldn't last. I grieved over our 2 month relationship as if it had been 2 years and I did it in silence because no one understood what I felt. How could I feel what I felt with knowing someone for such a short period of time? We were like a married couple in love. We made out in the supermarket and held hands and our turn on was just being together. We never went out and did anything. One night we went to In and Out Burgers. As we sat inside and waited for our food we kissed and cuddled like there was no one more important. I believe we both needed to have that feeling. I was in love with Bishop and I didn't care who knew it. He took care of me. In two months we had even gotten to the point of private jokes and pet names. I even knew that he wiggled his toes when he woke up or before he went to sleep.

We fit together like a hand in a glove. We always had to be touching some part of our bodies even if it was nothing but our fingers. There were times when we had withdrawals like drug heads because his daughter was at his house and we couldn't see each other. It was so intense we were ready to do almost anything to see each other. I can remember driving over to his house in the middle of the night just to stand outside so we could hug each other. We actually looked like the perfect couple. When we hugged and looked in the mirror we looked great together. I am now thinking of how long it has taken him to get my picture off of his phone or if he has taken it off. We are now three months shy of a year since we last spoke.

I always remember his birthday of January 16th because it was the day my grandmother died. And his age is the same as my oldest brother. He was my Big Daddy.

My feelings for him were obvious because I slept with him and I hadn't been with a man in over 2 years. Oh yeah, the first day I met him he was wearing Curve cologne. I had been out of the game for so long that the entire ride from San Francisco to Berkeley I was trying to figure out the fragrance. Before we went in the store I figured it out and that is one of my favorites. I felt good like I had been awakened from a long sleep and my prince at that time was Bishop.

As I have sat here writing for the past hours, I realize what I thought was tired were just thoughts weighing on my mind. Now I'm not tired anymore. My past is really on my mind and it brings up so many buried emotions. As we know, they don't go away. They're just waiting for you to push the right button and the memories will come back as clear as day. Like I said before, that is what I know for sure is whatever you're feeling for a person, they are feeling it for you. So all of these men I sit here remembering are remembering me too, even Mo Mo. I know he thinks of me too. After Bishop left then came Mo Mo.

I truly believe had I not taken those pills I would have been pregnant by Bishop. God gave me the good foresight to get the "morning after" pills and I didn't even have to pay for them. I got them just in a nick of time. I think it would have worked out the same way as my marriage. Even though he wanted me to get pregnant he would have been mad that I did. We actually had talks about in vitro and if I would consider it. He was confused. Bishop loved me and probably still does.

Now I know why when you're making love with your man you

are so often times led to call out for God. Because it is at that time that you're having a spiritual connection He intended you to have while making love. These men that I mention, including Troy, have taken me to that place of being close to God and for that I will always remember them and they will always remember me.

It will be such a pleasure to have that experience with my God fearing, devout Christian and loving husband. I know God already has him picked out for me, but I have to continue along on my journey to get to him. He is on his journey as well. He is as spiritually in tuned as I am and he is going to follow God and He will put us together and we will know. We both are spiritually in tuned enough to know when a union is from God. Both our journeys are preparing us for the meeting so we'll have the heightened enough awareness to know.

August 9, 2007—Thursday—7:43pm

This has been another awesome day serving God. I woke up today knowing my message from God was to do all of the things He has put on my heart to do.

I have truly experienced the energy release that takes place during the process of giving. When I gave Tyler the apology it lifted a burden from my body. I guess that was guilt I had been carrying around. Today when I gave Tony the gift of forgiving him and wishing him well was another freeing experience for me. Even when I called and left the message for Alan Case and gave the apology on his work voicemail, I still felt the same freeing feeling as if I had done it in person. I know he will get the message I have given. I also felt it again when I gave away my crystal candle stick holders and brand new glasses and punch bowl. Whoever gets those items from my laundry room will wonder what is going on. How could someone give away such beautiful items and want nothing in return?

It's just like what Tony said, "You get it back ten-fold." When I called him today I hoped that he would not answer the phone but he did. I immediately told him what my reason was for calling—that it was to wish him well. I could hear in his voice what I said to him almost brought tears to his eyes. What I was really doing was saying, I forgive you.

After the day we saw each other I knew he had time to reflect on our past relationship and I know there are some parts of that nightmare he had to remember clearly. Just as I went through my thoughts about my relationship with Tyler, I didn't remember everything, but what I did remember was hurtful enough that I could only imagine the rest. It had to have come back to Tony the same way.

When I called him today, he didn't apologize to me for anything, but I can tell by his response to me that the weight of my well wishes was so powerful because of who it was coming from. He gave it right back to me with a heartfelt thank you and mentioned my timing could not have been better. My well wishes penetrated his spirit and were received with my full intention. With a huge amount of force he wished it upon me ten-fold.

Tony underneath was not a bad person. He just was not aware of the impact of a lot of the choices he made. I can see now that he has grown and he now understands the value of good people.

It's almost like the situation with Tyler. I appreciated him when we were together, but it wasn't until all of these years later that I really got it. It did his heart a wealth of good to know I truly appreciate him. With Tony I know he gets it. He now values me as a person. He knows I loved him then and I love him now and the value of this is immeasurable. When he asked me how I was doing I felt compelled to tell him everything was great just as Tyler had done for me. Just as it would have brought my spirit down to think anything less. He gave me the gift of making me believe everything was great in his world. My good sense tells me it's not. He had a limp. I'm not sure of his business situation and he didn't get hyped about his birthday the way we used to back in the day.

I gave the same gift to Tony by not mentioning any of the things I am working to overcome in my life. I made him feel better.

I feel like now I'm finally becoming a free person in my life. Free from guilt and shame and all I have been carrying around with me for all of these years. Now all I have to do is continue to move through life in a good way and all will be well.

It's so funny that for as much as I loved Tony I'm not going through the agony I experienced over Tyler or even Alan. When I thought deeply about them I was overwhelmed by my feelings for the love we shared. Maybe it's because Tony was only taking in the relationship and that is nothing to long for.

Tyler and Alan loved me. They both told me and showed me in every way.

When I look at where I am today I know it's exactly where I'm supposed to be because God has had a chance to reach me. If I had been working somewhere all of these exact occurrences would not have taken place at that exact time. Even if you're not a Godly person you would have to know this whole thing is not an accident. I truly feel I am getting closer to the meaning of all of this. The responses I'm getting to the messages that I'm giving are very unexpected and a bit overwhelming. I am currently sowing some good seeds that are about to produce a harvest that as they say will not be able to be stored in my barn. If the responses I'm getting are any indication to what is coming my way and they say ten times over—I will need to have God's strength to help me to handle all of my blessings.

August 10, 2007—Friday—1:08am

I can tell by Peaches' response by saying her auntie was on the phone that I was right to call and explain to her the meaning of the heart necklace and ink pen that I gave her. I wanted her to know the man that gave me the necklace gave it to me, in love, about twenty years ago when I was her age. I held on to it for all of these years and I was passing it on to her in love. I explained to her even though she is not my brother's biological daughter that I claim her consistently and even publicly as my niece and as my family. The hearts I have given to her are to remind her of that. I told her when my brothers and I were growing up we all had different fathers and sometimes that could make things pretty interesting. I told her I understood and that she is my niece. I also told her through the softness of my voice that the young man who had given me that necklace and heart pendant all of those years ago—I saw him the other day. Also I realize after all of this time he still loves me and I still love him. I had to tell him before I left town I had given the necklace to her. I definitely wanted to let her know it was not just a piece of jewelry, but it was a piece of someone's heart.

I told Ms. Be Be that she reminded me of my mother with her quiet spirit and that I too have a quietness about me. I also told her it took some time for me to figure out it was okay to be that way. I told her it was okay for her to keep her feelings and thoughts to herself and not share them with other people because they don't always understand.

I lastly spoke to Ms. Carlotta and apologized to her for saying she wasn't helping out around the house. I let her know her father told me she was doing her part and my reason for even saying anything to her was out of concern for her mother. I closed by telling her to just keep being who she is and I would talk to her later.

August 10, 2007—Friday—4:24am

When I woke up a couple of hours late, I didn't want to, but I got up and brushed my teeth and flossed and put in my braces. I did it because I have been doing those things every night no matter what for the past weeks and I'm trying to get used to the new habit. I got up out of my sleep and did these things because it was my way of fighting off the devil because he wants me to not take care of my teeth. Taking care of my teeth is another thing I do unto God to show Him I am grateful for what I have.

When I woke up I had a little nagging headache and I know it's because I thought I had figured out some part of my journey and God has just proven to me I have not. I just have to keep listening to Him and obeying Him. I do have to admit I really want to know where I'm being led. He is also letting me know to not worry about this rent thing. Somehow an angel has stepped in and taken care of it for me like they did the bill for the clinic shots. These things are far beyond what I could have ever imagined possible. I am just grateful and quiet about this rent situation. Like Pastor William says, don't look a gift horse in the mouth.

Last Sunday he mentioned one of the principles of good financial management is to know how much you owe. I really felt like he was speaking to me because I can see someone coming up to me and asking me that question in order to satisfy my debts. I need to be prepared for it. I say that too because he was so confident while explaining the mission program to me even though I have debt. He was very serious when he said, it could be taken care of like the other debt. If he knows I am just that committed to serving God, the church may help me get rid of my debt.

I am right now feeling a little sick to my stomach and with a headache because of all of this. God is in control and I have to wait on Him. God is an amazing God. He is creative and always finds a way to get the job done. After all of this is done I will have to share with Be Be how she was a part of my destiny. God used her sweet little self to help her auntie along her journey and I can't think of a more perfect niece for the job.

I feel like I'm so close to this thing I can taste it. I think that's what's making me sick—the anticipation. I wonder if I will know by the time I finish this journal which is not long from now looking at how much writing I'm doing. It seems to make sense because it would be a fresh start, so it would be appropriate to have a new book. I believe I'm really getting closer because my messages are getting closer and louder. I'm getting them more frequently and more in your face. God is hot on the case and I must be patient and wait for my assignment from Him.

I feel like I'm in the twilight zone experiencing things that are really happening but are unimaginable to the human mind. These things are really happening to me and I can't wait to share them with the world, but even Ray Charles can see it is not to be now. I'm smart enough to know better and not even attempt to go there with anyone. I could tell Pastor William, but I'll wait until it has run its course and I get the final results. I'm so glad for him that he will get to witness this miracle in his lifetime and in his career and with one of his parishioners. It will re-energize him to help him to continue on in his ministry knowing his work is not in vain. If it had not been for him, I wouldn't be where I am. He helped to grow me up in the Lord. I think he might even cry when he finds this out— knowing him.

I can see I must journal because I must get these things out of me. This has helped my headache to go away and it helps to keep track of these events for later reference. It's also helping me to grow in my use of the English language because I notice it even comes out in my speech.

Hey, I haven't even dealt with the Laura Conway part of the story, but I know it's coming because she is due back at school next week and she might have been taking a vacation for the summer as some teachers do. My feet are looking pretty great these days and that means a ton.

August 12, 2007—Sunday—11:18pm

Today I went to see Mrs. Houston to give her some flowers. Her caregiver told me she was not doing too well. But she seemed all there to me. Mrs. Houston complimented me on my outfit and high heel shoes.

When I told her about her great grandchildren, especially Stacy, she described her as sophisticated. I told her I had not thought of it that way. She did not remember who I was, but when I mentioned Bobby was my brother she got very excited and started flapping her arms and kept giving me hugs and kept saying he was a gentleman and such a nice young man. She mentioned she had just been thinking about him the night before and she called him by his first and middle name. I hoped he would call her soon because I had just told him on the Thursday before I felt led to tell him to call her. This is how she spoke of him even the first time I saw her.

Upon my first visit we sat and talked for hours and she joyfully remembered the past. She remembered her childhood friend. She mimicked how the little girl would run around her house to the windows and the door calling out her name Sweetie or Sweetie Pie—asking if she could come out to play.

She told me she was from Houston, Texas and said that Galveston was the place for fun. She said sometimes when she had the blues she would get on the bus and ride to Galveston where it was swingin' and jumpin'. She even stomped her foot and slapped her hand on her knee while saying this. She said Galveston was the place to have a good time.

She recalled her uncle Baby Boy and that he boxed and how he had come to California. She mentioned she finally moved from Texas with her husband Mr. Houston. She said her husband decided they should come to California because he wanted his sons to have the opportunity to be addressed as a man and not a boy.

She gave me words of wisdom, like be patient with people because we're all different. Be careful how you talk to people, and do unto others as you would have them do unto you. The thing she kept repeating and it was probably what I needed to hear... was to listen and don't talk so much. She even got a kick out of saying, "Nothing runs a duck but his bill."

We had a great time that day. I sat and listened to her relive her days from the past and share things that were on her mind and things that brought her joy. The one thing that really stood out for me was toward the end of our visit she sat up in her chair and gracefully crossed her legs and put her hand to her face and with total finesse looked at me and said, "I'm a Texas Lady."

She was very observant even from across the room. She told me I must be a very particular person because of the whiteness of my tennis shoes and the arching of my eyebrows. She even mentioned how she remembered a time when she used to arch hers. This was another time when you could hear the joy in her voice and see the light in her eyes and the smile on her face.

Remembering was a happy experience. This was proof she has lived a good life.

The fact that she couldn't remember who I was and yet was so complimentary and entertaining and so gracious a host says a lot. Her heart was just the way I remembered it. She didn't have a judging bone in her body and just as when I was a kid making childhood mistakes—she made me still feel the same way, welcome. I guess people don't really change—do they? The essence of a person remains intact no matter what else leaves them. This was a blessing to see and experience. All these years later she is still so full of love.

God did create an angel in this Texas Lady.

August 15, 2007—Wednesday—5:52am

I feel great. I can say I have hope again today. Yesterday morning I read the God's Timing book Alejandra gave me and it was right on. I really believe what God has called me to do is to go into the ministry and start a church. This mirrors the idea of starting a school. I would still be a missionary because I would be preaching God's word and not drawing a salary from it. I could substitute teach during the day for income and preach on Saturday evenings.

I believe God is leading me to talk to the people at the recreation center on Parker. My next choice would be Carver in The Town. I first thought of Parker because of all of the people wandering around down there and they would then have a place to go. Even the people from the Safe Place could come on down. That would be rewarding work. I would just focus on the preaching because when you start trying to do everything else like feed people, you don't know if they're coming for that or the Word. I want to offer nothing but the Word for now.

I could go to that area and talk to the people and pass out flyers and tell them to make sure to come. I could play my brother Caleb's CD. I think it is really special and I could tell the people the music is his. I could start off with the music to get everyone in the mood and then get into my story. I'd thank everyone for coming and tell them where I'm from, about the rape, the drugs, the men and how God saved me when I didn't even know Him. I could tell them about my family, my mother's mental health issues, that my brothers and I all have different fathers, but both of them live and work on the right side of the law. Also one of them has already retired from an admirable career with 20 years of service—and how bad he used to be. I'd bring them up to date and tell them how I graduated from high school in summer school. Then God helped me to graduate from college twice while each time losing a parent. As kids we ate a lot of toast for meals and cereal with water. And my first job was at a thrift store.

I'm believing this is what God wants me to do. Monday I was reading a magazine which focused on starting new churches. I noticed everyone had a pastoral degree from a particular Christian college, even if they worked as a pastor in a converted night club. It was always made clear the person was formally educated. I even notice at my church everyone is totally educated.

So my next thought was, how does God want me to do this without credentials and all of the other stuff you need? When I got up and turned on Joyce's program she started talking about stuff that made no sense according to the title of the program or topic she was on. She said clearly, your mess can be your message and your ministry and you are authorized and anointed because you are called by God to do this. I was in shock because it seemed like she was talking directly to me, specifically to my heart. I think that day it even brought tears to my eyes and that is always my sign from God.

In the magazine it talks about the pastor doing everything himself–even having a day job. All of the articles even talked about going into the worst neighborhoods. Automatically I envisioned the Parker Center area and I thought of using it because they have electricity. That whole population down there is a good size meeting. I would be so glad to see them take a chance on me—believing I might have something to say worth hearing. Just like they say in the magazine, I would be after the people who would be uncomfortable in church. This is another thing Joyce mentioned on TV. Those are the people you want to reach. All of my concerns and thoughts, she spoke to them when I turned on the TV. This is how I know it was God. The reason why He had me to go through this whole process is because there was a part of me that wanted to do it for the show, before. He humbled me to know I am ready to do whatever for Him, even go into the worst neighborhood.

Caleb must really not be all that bad if he is willing to pick-up men from the Safe Place and take them to church every weekend, faithfully. He is serving the Lord. I just wish the Lord could heal his heart a little more so he can have a better life.

I know in my heart this is what God wants me to do and I believe I am now supposed to totally resign from the school district because I don't think it's appropriate to do both. I will need freedom. That is why it would be good for me to substitute through an agency because I would be all over. Maybe after I got comfortable with this, I could go to other places to speak to supplement my income. That is also what one guy did in the magazine.

Yesterday I stood in my doctor's office and had to push back the tears because of all of the things that are happening in my life. They are good things, but I know there is so much change just around the corner. The lady in the doctor's office said it is just the fear of the unknown. I told her I could feel it happening while I was standing there at that moment. A clue to that was how the day had gone so far.

When I called Stephen in the morning he said he'd be about 45 minutes and he'd be at the storage place and James would help. It was just enough time for James to help before he got on the plane. Stephen's timing gave me enough time to go and print the thing I had written for him and close out my storage account before I met with him. He and James did all of the work. All I had to do was hold or open doors.

When we got the furniture in my house, I could see it really looked nice. When we got downstairs after finishing, I was talking to James about my possible new project of starting a church. He was supportive and surprised. It was a joy meeting him. He has so much going for him and he is my cousin.

After they left I went upstairs and had to figure out what to do with myself, so I called the temp agencies to let them know I'm still available for work.

After that I decided to call Dr. Wilmington's office to find out if I could come in earlier than my 4pm appointment. That was when I realized I had mixed up the times and should have been there at 9am instead. I was so embarrassed and because they don't have my home number they couldn't have called me the day before to remind me. Oh my goodness. They were at lunch and not answering the phone, so I had time to take a shower, with my stinky self. By the time I got out of the shower and called them they said to come on in. I had time to get dressed and all was well.

After getting there I talked to Dr. Wilmington and he told me it was good I didn't come at 9am because he had to do an emergency surgery. That was when I really knew the shift I had just read about in the God's Timing book was happening. Everything was falling into place just too perfectly.

My reality was, I could take the furniture instead of paying the bill. This saved me from stressing over a bill I didn't have the money for. The day I took it out James was in town and hadn't taken his flight so he could help. Even when I called Stephen to schedule it he had just walked in the house. The delay we had yesterday with meeting gave me time to print the write-up and settle my account. When I got to the doctor's office late in the day it was perfect because he couldn't have seen me anyway. If I had known I had that appointment I would not have scheduled with Stephen for the time I did. It would have been too close to my dental appointment then we would have missed James and everything would not have gone as smoothly. That dental appointment mix up is what really helped me to know the shift was occurring now. Like right now.

Like the woman advised me to do when you've had enough—just go to bed and deal with everything later. I called and left a voicemail for Troy before I went to the dentist which was an hour before he told me to call. By the time I got home he didn't answer at all and his phone went directly to voicemail. He does know what I need and I need it now because I told him so. Either he doesn't want to tell me no or he has something else going on. Either way, I still care for him because I know his situation. My new understanding is sometimes it's hard to say hard things to people so you just don't say anything. I think I can understand because I've been in that situation myself and I didn't want to tell the hurtful truth.

I am really trying not to stress about my rent and what's going to happen next in my life. I had a lot on my mind so I ate some peanut butter because when I got on the scale I was more than 155 pounds which is wicked. I put on Joyce who was discussing missed opportunities and I fell asleep.

When I woke up I felt 200 times better. I rearranged my living room and cleaned mother's furniture and listened to Caleb's CD over and over again—because I plan on using it for my service. I have timed it to see how long it is. It's the perfect music for what I want to do. The fact that it's my brother's really makes it the right music for my ministry.

I truly believe I'm supposed to stay here and start a ministry. But I had to have to apply for the Trinity job so God could have a way of communicating with me—seeing as I don't watch TV. He had to have me to learn that I could write a sermon and applying for all of those jobs showed me that. He had to tell me I was going to Africa so I could get the perfect combination of shots to cure my thyroid problem. Also so I could have the cure and the bill settlement for my testimony. He had to tell me to get rid of my things because I had to make room for what was best. Now I have mother's furniture in my home. What an honor. Now I have a prayer corner I didn't have before. And now God has made the entire place more spiritual instead of just my bedroom. He has shown me that Freda Kahlo must go because she had a tortured spirit and never thought she was good enough. God told me her time was up by breaking the glass on her picture. It is much too beautiful to destroy so He said it's time to give it away. Diego can stay because his picture radiates love and he was confident as an artist. His other flaws were just human flaws. I will find a picture that radiates love for my bathroom and I think it's time to maybe put up mother's towels or at least change what's there—to start anew.

It's almost like I am having a fresh start in my home and it will be also in my career. It's all in how you see things. As I scrubbed mother's furniture it reminded me of what had taken place between my brothers and myself. We had not talked to each other for over ten years and now all is well. We don't speak often, but at least I can call either of them and tell them I love them and it would be returned. That furniture is a symbol of what is possible in life. It is so strong and sturdy and unique that it truly represents the spirit of my mother. That is who she was.

Even though she was a quiet woman, she had something special about her because the clothes she wore took a huge amount of boldness that I don't have. God even pulled an Abraham on me and told me to sell her furniture and jewelry and He was just testing my obedience to Him—because He didn't really want me to.

The items I got rid of—it was time to let them go. Most of the jewelry I gave to the nieces was from people who cared about me and loved me, but that was in the past. Moving into my future those items needed to go to someone else to enjoy. Releasing those items also helped me to release old feelings of guilt and shame. So this was a part of my necessary healing. The black pearls were the perfect gift for Harriet and the trade for the bracelet was needed. Because I have seen a light in that woman's eyes since I gave her that jade heart. I guess God knew she needed it. I didn't have to give up the jewelry I wear everyday that my brother gave me or figure out what to do about grandmother's hats. I was able to hold on to my pimp suits also.

When I bought them I envisioned myself standing in front of people in church speaking in those suits. That's why I bought so many. I guess this will come true.

God had to get my heart ready for the work He wants me to do. He needed my heart to be more pure. And Eloise just talked herself out of the box because at this stage in the game—you are either for me or against me. Anyone suspected of not being on my team is forgotten. I really feel comfortable with my decision about Eloise and Darrell because it goes back to how they make me feel. She actually was saying it out of her mouth. I think this split frees up some space for me. It's one less obligation and I don't have to be phony. They are not my parents, but if they acted more the part then it would be different. They don't understand me and I can't go to them if I really need them—so for me it's a play or pretend relationship. But they want all of the kudos of being called mom and dad. I don't think so. You have to give to get and they don't want to give what it would take to get what they want. The pretend relationship is too much energy for me. It's also too painful to watch the development or lack of for that boy. They don't love me as much as they love him.

I think the shift with making Bobby the beneficiary for my life insurance has actually strengthened our relationship. It lets him know even though I don't talk to you all of the time—I am giving him the most important responsibility I can right now. I'm sure it made him feel really proud because I could hear it in his voice. His response was, "Sure I'll be the man." I also know he is working on his situation over there because of Scriptures I've given him. I know he'll see the things I've given the kids and also that I gave the girls jewelry. He can tell I'm committed to the cause of serving the Lord.

As they say, I know He didn't bring me this far to leave me.
So God is going to come through with something for this rent. I have now made a new home for myself with His help. He wants me to exercise my hope and faith muscles and all will be well.

I also don't see God leading me in the direction of the foster care thing anymore because I would have to go buy everything I just gave away and that would be crazy. It was just a part of the process to get me where I am today—open to serve God in my highest possible way. Everything was for Mo Mo to come into my life and make a change in me. It worked as God's plans always do. You may not understand, but just do what He wants you to do and it always works out for your good.

Oh yeah, I'm now going to put a stop payment on that passport check and get the money. I might as well get this off of my chest. When I start doing this ministry thing, I believe I'm going to have to quit my church. It doesn't make sense for the pastor of one church to be a member of another unless it's a parent church and it won't be. It goes back to what you're doing in the community and who it affects. I wouldn't want anyone to think I was representing that church and he wouldn't either because all of their people are credentialed. I believe he would bless what I'm doing but understand my having to leave. I won't make it to the new church that is being built and that was something I wondered about. I knew this was coming—that there was going to be this big change in my life coming.

Oh yeah, the Carson Trinity thing was a test to see if I would put my life out there for all to see, for Him. This was something else to see if I was ready to serve Him in the way He has planned for me. I'm looking forward to the rest of the journey. When I talk to Pastor William he will be surprised, but he won't.

August 16, 2007—Thursday—7:12am

I am now going to take a nap because I am very tired. I have been up following God's instructions to continue cleaning up my stuff. I have been shredding and sorting for four hours. But when I got to the next to the last book of a stack, I got my clue that I'm on the right track.

One may not think so because my rent is due today and Bobby was not able to help. I pulled a Joyce move and asked for a lot that way if I got anything or even that amount it would be great. I asked for three thousand dollars. It didn't hurt at all that he was not able because I know it's just a part of God's design. The same amount I asked for is the same amount for Peaches' tuition he had just paid. What a coincidence.

After I got off the phone with him I went to sorting and shredding. It was just when I had enough is when God's clue showed me I was exactly where He wanted me to be. That was a big relief because of course I reviewed everything in my mind to make sure I had done everything He has asked me. Even yesterday I spent money on food and detergent and about twenty dollars on a serenity prayer picture. Before I saw it I was about to walk out of the store, but as sure as I'm sitting here something told me to turn around and there it was.

Even though it was more than what I planned on spending, it had my name written all over it. That is what I had been trying to get on that bracelet. So I bought it and took it home. Even the cashier at the store was very afraid to touch it because it was as if she knew the significance of it. It was the perfect thing to replace Freda. I was looking for a totally different energy and found it.

When I got it home I wasn't all that sure because I wasn't able to use mother's towels as planned. But I finally found the right combination and it works. I even found myself walking over to it from the living room after talking to God to recite that serenity prayer because I really needed that message. Do all that I can do and leave the rest to God.

I asked my brother for the money. Now I will ask Auntie and I think I will be able to get it from her because she always has something stashed. The funny thing about her is even though she can be funny, she makes me feel worth it in that she will do whatever she can. This is what I mean about Eloise and Darrell. I know to not even ask them. Because they make me feel like I'm not good enough to go out on a limb for. They make you feel like $40 is a bankroll. Like everything hurts.

My horoscope for the day says that it's gonna be a great day of great luck, from love, to a windfall of money based on all of the good karma I've sown. The timing would be perfect, but that's the way I expect it to happen—because that's how I gave it, generously, and in a nick of time.

It's all going to work out.

I also believe God wants me to take a long term assignment or at least open myself up to it since I'm going to be here. We will see how this big day unfolds. I thank God for everything because it all works out for the good. Bobby told me to ask Caleb for help, but I don't wanna make him feel bad because if he can't that would hurt his own feelings. I want him to be happy. I hope my letter helped. I'm sure it did. He's very sentimental and he would appreciate the fact that I took the time to do something so personal and special for him. I know he was on cloud nine when he got it. I had to let him read it by himself because God wasn't trying to let me feel my flesh. It was only for him and not for me too. God sure is a funny one. He even made it so I couldn't put those pictures in there because they might have changed the dynamics of the whole paper. The message and intention was clear without the pictures. Good job for stopping me from messing up.

August 17, 2007—Friday—7:39am

I am working on fumes by now. I was very productive yesterday. I only have one box left and it's the one with all of the cards and stuff. I shredded and searched the internet for seminary information as well as ordination information. After all of this, I have finally asked Harriet if she can share her information.

After a pretty good slumber yesterday, I woke up and called Auntie and asked her for the money I needed for my rent. I actually have to call her again today because God has spoken to my heart about the extra money she gave me. I have to call to let her know the actual amount of my rent. I don't know if I intentionally misled her or not, but I have to clear that up because I can't have anything messing with my anointing. I'm sure she'll be okay about it, but I really have to do this to maintain a good relationship with God. That is the most important thing to me. But again, I'm sure she will be okay with it. She volunteered information about Carmen helping people to find a job. So I told her I would call her today, as tired as I was. I made sure I kept my word and called Carmen.

Before I called her I had been looking up theological schools and it was even still on the computer screen when I called her. We got to talking and something told me to go ahead and share. All of the things she was talking about were things God has spoken to me about doing. These things ranged from leaving my job, to publishing a book, to preaching the gospel and getting a theological degree. I was too freaked out by what she was saying. I knew she was telling the truth because how could her story have matched mine so precisely. She even rounded off the story about all of these other women who are in different fields but putting Christianity first. One woman is even preaching at a YWCA and another is doing it on the radio.

If I had put that phone call off for another day—who knows. You know how people are in a difference mood at different times and actually the next day would have been Friday and that really is a whole different energy. She did say missionary work and to not get too comfortable because there would be movement. That's what I feel about me. I believe job situations could vary with my ministry, but my living quarters will be pretty stable.

This really did happen overnight. On Monday, I got the confirmation and on Thursday I got validation this is what I'm supposed to do. Even Bobby said that. I didn't tell him what it was exactly, but I told him about the mirrored conversation and he said it was confirmation from God about what I'm supposed to do. One thing I did hear her say is that employment for money is important and she doesn't tell people what she's doing because they might try to discourage her. She has had to make some hard choices she knows were best for her.

I question if I should really tell people before I start. I know I won't tell anyone at Crenshaw. She did confirm that I'll need to quit my job with the school district because it would be a conflict of interest. She even said that with a deep—now, as in you really need to go. I will take care of it on Monday. I won't tell anyone my plans.

God has even given me the vision of what the service looks like and I already have my music. This morning I realized my closing song is Until I See You Again. It is the most perfect song. It's almost like how Happy Trails is the perfect good-bye song. It is sung by a woman and it is slow and heartfelt. It has a prayer in it that says I hope to see you again. After I took the time to get into it, I stood up and looked in the mirror and imagined myself singing it to the congregation with a smile on my face and my hand in the air. I could see them feeling it as well with hands in the air and ending the service on a positive note. I believe whoever showed up would enjoy it. To be honest with myself, I'm wondering what to do about too many people. I know this is ordained by God so I know they will show. Everything God has put inside of me—like the love and joy and humor and directness and the feeling of the words will show. The people will know I'm sincere and that will bring them back for the love.

When regular people show up for church it's just not such a big deal because they've heard a lot of the stuff already. And whatever their barriers are they don't really keep them from functioning in society. But when the obviously wounded come in and sit and give you their attention, God has to show up so He can show off. He has a point to prove that He is worth it and that He can take such a wounded soul and make it smile and give it hope that maybe today is a new day—with the help of the Lord. They will know for sure. We would definitely have to offer the Sinner's Prayer or something to give people an opportunity to change their lives. This is what makes me want to have some type of officialness to myself because it's an honor to help usher people into a relationship with the Lord. I can see people driving down the street and wondering where are all of the lost souls that are usually wandering the street. They would be inside trying to get some of God's love and fill up on it. Soon it would be their new drug of choice.

You know how they say, if it's good enough the first time you can get hooked right then. We know God can do it. His spirit can fill a room and touch you inside in a place you thought was dead. When I think of what could happen, I better have an anointed person there with me to help. This has happened so fast. What if as soon as I walk in the place, the Parker Center, things just fall into place?

The one thing I know for sure is the message is going to be—God loves them and that will be the point of my story. I want to tell about all of the times God saved my life—when I didn't even know who He was. He still loved me. That's what people are truly looking for—is love. My message is not going to be—they should change, but God loves you just the way you are. But when you change on the inside it will make you want to change on the outside.

August 22, 2007—Wednesday—1:12am

This is probably the last entry for this journal and I think it's appropriate. Tomorrow I will have one of the most serious and important conversations in my life. I am going to meet with Pastor William Walker to discuss my future relationship with the church.

I am going to tell him I had been informed by God it is now time for me to discontinue my membership with the church. This is solely based on opening another door to serve God. When I present myself to the world it needs to be as just a child of God willing to serve Him to the fullest. I believe God also wants me to start my own ministry, but He wants to have full direction and control over how it is run. He wants me to answer only to Him.

As I sit here now writing this, it comes back to me so clearly the prior circumstances I was in. God had me running my own ministry within someone else's ministry and it was the worst feeling I've ever had in my life. That situation also caused a lot of dissention between members of the church. It was a very bad situation, but I do believe there were some students who benefited. If the situation had been different, there could have been lots more and this is why God wants me to do it on my own. So He can speak to me and guide me in the way He sees fit without having to be stifled by someone's preferences.

I know God wants to use me and He has shown and proven that to me. But He hasn't made it totally clear as of yet, exactly how. I believe one thing He needed to know was if I would follow all of His wishes and I have proven to Him I will. I was willing to sell my mother's jewelry and furniture and even go to Africa. Those were all tests for me just like Abraham. He tested Abraham's obedience with his beloved son Isaac to see if he would sacrifice him.

Now God knows for sure I will be obedient to Him no matter what. He will open the door He wants me to walk through. This obedience will be proven by my willingness to leave my church I love so much. The church and pastor who have fed me and raised me up to a mature adult. They have given me enough knowledge and strength to be able to go out into the world and survive and now have something to share with others.

I see myself right now moving through time not believing it's really me, like this is all happening to someone else. I believe the principles of reaping and sowing are truly evident in my life. I knew my aunt would give me the money she did because I had just done it for someone else. I really wasn't shocked that she gave me extra. Again, because I had done the same thing for someone else.

Yesterday while I was waiting for the maintenance person to come, I went to the trash to throw out some watermelon rinds and lo and behold there was a dining room set sitting near the trash area. It was just like what I had pictured in my mind a couple of days ago. I imagined something with clear glass so it would not be too much of a main focus in the room. I wanted a couple of chairs because it's just reasonable to have them because I always have to stand up to use the telephone. The dinette set was also made of the black metal that matches my bookcase, computer stand and TV stand. On top of all of that the cushions were black with gold spots to match all of the gold items in my apartment. This could not have been better if I had done it myself. On top of all of that, it was small enough for me to pick it up and carry it myself and it didn't cost me a dime. So I was a witness to someone giving just like I had. I gave away nice items and it caused someone to turn around and do the same thing and I was the one to benefit. I had reaped that which I had sown and I really did need a table. The funny thing about it is it had good energy in it. It smells like a man's cologne and the sweater he was also giving away was folded so neatly and placed on the top of the table, like it was done with care. This same gentleman put out some shoes and boxes yesterday. The white tennis shoes he gave away were almost new, clean and barely warn.

The three days I spent out on 32nd street talking to "out the way" Stanly Black at 56 years of age, gave me a new perspective on things. I now realize as a part of where I'm at in my journey I'm supposed to meet different people along the way. I will help them and they will help me to get to where I am supposed to go. While I was cleaning out my last box of shredible items of cards and things, I ran across a postcard from Sampson and it was a picture of Dorothy from the Wizard of Oz, standing on the yellow brick road. I guess that really is me. The funny thing about it is she was in the middle of San Francisco on her brick road. This is truly my story. And along the way she met the scare crow and the tin man and the lion and she helped them and they helped her.

That was the last box I went through and that card was in the last set of papers I grabbed. As always it was right on time even though it was mailed to me in 1999.

Now that I have rearranged my apartment and gotten a couple of new things I feel totally different about my apartment. I feel like it's a totally new experience. It's just like when I had the car accident and got my car painted. It now feels like a new car. I was so anxious to get out of my apartment and now I love it. It has a totally new and different feel to it. The energy has been changed and the young man who gave me that table I hope God will bless him. He is a good man.

Well, tomorrow is a big day and I look forward to what it has in store for me. I know doors are going to continue to open for me just like the day I quit my job. Three sub positions were offered to me and two people called or contacted me to let me know they hadn't forgotten about me. Within this twenty minute conversation with Pastor William tomorrow I have to close this door and then wait for the others to open. Because I followed God and visited Mrs. Houston's house—I was able to get the article about her caregiver's daughter, who as a doctor created a mechanism to help with female pelvic exams. On the cover of the article it says, "She Opened Her Own Doors." This is what God wants me to do. He wants me to do something that's never been done before.

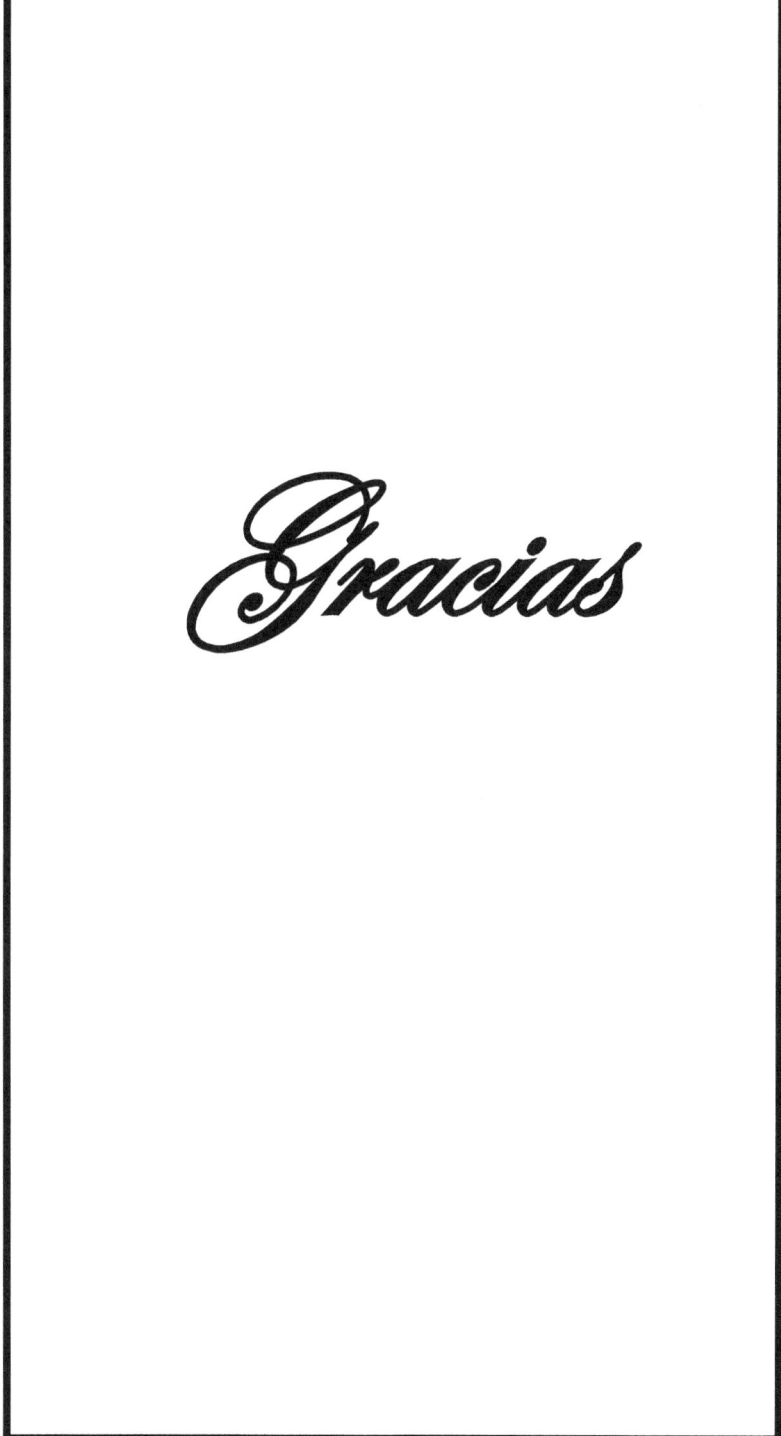

www.ingramcontent.com/pod-product-compliance
Lightning Source LLC
Chambersburg PA
CBHW060532100426
42743CB00009B/1506